THE WALLACES OF ALABAMA

The
WALLACES
of
ALABAMA

MY FAMILY, by George Wallace, Jr.
as told to James Gregory

With a Special Introduction by
Gov. George C. Wallace of Alabama

Follett Publishing Company · Chicago

Library of Congress Catalog Card Number: 74–24573
ISBN: 0–695–80528–2

SECOND PRINTING

This Book Is Dedicated
To the Memory of My Mother,
Gov. Lurleen Burns Wallace
of Alabama

Introduction

By Gov. George C. Wallace of Alabama

M Y SON GEORGE has had a somewhat difficult time, as most sons and daughters of people in public life have had, because their parents have had to be away so much. You find as time goes by that you wish you had been able to be in public life and still spend full time with your children.

But George is clean-cut and serious. He's intelligent. He's quiet. He's really not an extrovert; he's more of an introvert. In fact, I wish he were a little bit more outgoing. But maybe that will come.

How do I feel about his musical career? Well, I would like for George to seek whatever career he would enjoy, one in which he could contribute something.

But I do want him to continue his education, because everybody doesn't hit it off in the field of music. Everybody's not a success. And whether he's going to be a success remains to be seen, although he's off to a fine start. I think he can continue in his effort toward a musical career while acquiring an education.

So I urged him to go back to school, after dropping out of the University of Alabama in the middle of his sophomore year to follow a musical career. And he *is* back in college now. Whatever he does, he can do it better with a basic educational background.

George has always been close to the family, and he was especially close to his mother. He has told me that after he graduates from college he hopes he can come back and help me in my work in some way. And I appreciate that.

Really, this is what he has said he wanted to do: He realizes my condition is that of a paralytic. And as I grow older, he knows that the time is coming, if I live that long, that I will be even more dependent on someone to aid me. And he's talked about coming back and helping look after me in *that* way.

But while it would be good to be living *near* him, he's going to have his own future, and his own family to look after, and he's not going to be able to look after *me*. In fact, I would not want him burdened with having to stay with me.

I would rather for him to be independent and on his own. If he stays in proximity to me, so that it's not far away to go to see him, that'll be great. But if he's not—well, he's got to live his own life.

I want my children to do what they want. It's always nice, naturally, for them to come and stay with you and around you. But they shouldn't be dependent on you, and you shouldn't be dependent on them.

As for his helping me in politics—and he's talked about that, too—any intelligent person can help you in anything. But I don't want George to get into politics just because *I've* been in politics. Because I don't think he would like to *be* in politics, as far as being a candidate is concerned, unless he changes his mind.

But if he changed his mind, I would certainly wish him well. I would naturally support my son in any endeavor he undertook.

I don't say that whatever he undertakes is going to be successful. In other words, he may not be successful in music, even though he's very talented. But, after all, that wouldn't be the end of the world.

In fact, it's hard for me to talk about things that might disappoint a young man, or disappoint *anybody:* some problem, or some calling or something that he wants to do and is not able to do. Because I now view things in a different perspective.

Before I was shot, I worried about things that seem *trivial* today, compared to the problem I now have of not being able to walk—not being a normal person, a normal human being in that particular regard.

I have adapted and accepted it, and am going to go ahead and not let it throw me. But if I could *walk* the next minute and be *whole* again, I would have no problem in the world, no worry in the world, save maybe the worry of losing a loved one in the family.

Whether I was Governor would make no difference.

Whether I had any money would make no difference.

If I was unemployed, I wouldn't worry about that one minute if I could walk again. Because that would be *trivial*.

So if George worries about his musical career now, if he worries about whether he's going to make it or not, it's really nothing to worry about.

Because if you *don't* make it, so what? It's not the end of the world. There are other ways. And as he grows older he will understand and realize that more.

I wasn't a winner in everything that *I* did in the beginning. I've been a loser at times. And you've got to *learn* to lose.

People ask how I've been able to face my injury without giving up and retreating into a shell. Well, I suppose the main reason has been that I had a family that encouraged me and stayed with me very closely. And that included George.

Had I been by myself—if my children were all away, and, my first wife having passed away, if I had not married again before I was injured—I don't know but what things might have been different. But I had a family that stayed very close and encouraged me.

Any trauma of this sort that you suffer brings you closer to your family, because you understand and realize your need for them more than you did before. When you're independent and on your own, sometimes you think you can make it alone. But I see now that I couldn't *make* it without my family. I'm lucky to have them.

And then, being a *known* person, when I was hurt I had much attention from people who live in our state and throughout the country, who encouraged me.

And I was involved in an activity that I considered

§ x §

to be of such a nature that I was making a contribution, and could continue to do so by coming back and getting well and serving out my term as Governor, and running again.

There are many things that you can see done in government that you can't see done anyplace else or *get* done anyplace else.

One, for instance, is a program for quads and paraplegics. It's a program of care once they leave the rehab centers, when they're not able to look after themselves. Alabama didn't *have* it until I got into this shape and saw the problems faced by these people who are out of sight and out of mind.

And, having been a victim myself—though fortunate enough to come back to a governor's mansion, where they could look after me—I now see the plight of some of these more clearly than I saw before.

But *I've* never *thought* about giving up. I have been *depressed* at times, but that's been months ago. I haven't had any depression in a *long* time. When you're in this shape, you just have to accept it, or indeed wither away in a shell and die. And I don't intend to do that.

I have been asked whether I've been inspired by Franklin Roosevelt's example in becoming President despite his paralysis. *Anybody* who has been successful in his field is inspiring, and especially someone in the same field that I am in, except that he was on a larger scale— he as President of the United States, and I as Governor of Alabama.

But it certainly made me know that being crippled doesn't keep you from serving as Governor. I function as well as Governor now as I did before I was shot.

Religion is always a comfort. In fact, I think that

has been one of the greatest comforters that I have had. And I think one reason I am living is because people, so many people, prayed for me.

We don't understand all that is in this universe, or how it works. But we have to have a little faith. And I feel that maybe I'm alive because sufficient prayers went up for me.

People ask me if I still hope that someday I may be able to walk again. I hope for a miracle and *pray* for a miracle. But medically, from a neurological standpoint, my doctors tell me I will not walk again.

I have *accepted* the fact that I will *not* walk. If I do walk, that's all to the good—something I will have gained. But I think the thing to do is to prepare and adapt yourself for the worst, which I have done, and pray and hope for the best.

Now let me tell you something about my son George when he was a little boy. I used to carry him swimming before he'd even started to school. He'd run me crazy every time he'd dive in, hollering, "Watch me, Daddy! Watch me!"

I can remember him falling once and busting his mouth. They had to take some stitches. It scared me to death.

He used to sit on my lap and pull my cigar out of my mouth when I wasn't looking—when I was watching TV or something—or when I'd light my "figfar," as he called the cigar.

I used to take him as a little fellow—four and five and six months old—put him in the front seat of the car and drive him up to the house of an old friend of mine, Billy Watson, and sit and let them nourish him, because I was very proud of him.

I used to carry him around to see *many* different people I'd visit. I'd just wrap him up and put him in the front seat of the car and lay him down. And I'd hold him with one hand and drive him up to a neighbor's house, as I did my daughters. I did Peggy that way, and I did Lee that way.

He went with me one time in '57 when I spoke to a big function in North Alabama, and we spent the night in Birmingham. He went to sleep at the banquet, and the mayor of the town up there set him in his lap. And he slept in the mayor's lap all the time I was making my talk.

Then he went to sleep in the car driving back to Birmingham. He got to the hotel room, called his mama, and went right off to sleep again. But he enjoyed that trip; he still remembers that we stayed in the Red Mountain Hotel.

Of course, I was away quite a bit during the time George was growing up. I was speaking and traveling, getting ready to run for Governor in 1958. And I remember that he was at the age where you always like to get back to young children, you know. . . .

I was running for Governor and he'd go down and visit his grandmother and grandfather, down in Greene County. Once I was speaking not far away in Pickens County, in an armory. That night I was tired, having spoken four or five times that day, and the weather being hot, and I got up on the stage to make a speech. And I looked down, and sitting right in the front row was George. And I could hardly speak, because I was so glad to see him. He doesn't remember that. But he was sitting right there with his grandpa and his grandma.

I never went hunting with George, but I went fishing with him. And we used to pass and punt and kick a football a lot in the backyard.

And, of course, I was going to baseball games and football games with him, and carried him to the school many times when he himself was playing. He played football when he was eleven and twelve years old, before and during my first term as Governor; I'd go out and watch him play every week here as Governor.

I watched him play Little League baseball, and he misjudged the first fly that came to him in the first game. When I reminded him of it recently, he said, "I needed *glasses*, really! And the lights were bright."

I don't do much "man-to-man" talking with George, but we are pretty close. And we were pretty close when he was a young fellow.

As he grew older, I was away a lot. But the life of a fellow who finally runs for the Governor's office necessitates a long-term expenditure of time: You travel 150 miles to speak to a club with 15 people in it, drive 100 miles to speak to one with 20 in it, then drive to the other end of the state to make an appearance. And I did that over a period of, you might say, fifteen years. I *lost* the *first* race for Governor in 1958, then won the second in 1962.

But George traveled with us on a lot of occasions in '58—he was a little fellow then—and in '62. In fact, in 1958 he spoke for me at rallies, although he was only six and seven years old. They'd have rallies in different counties where all the candidates for local offices would come, and they'd always keep him for last because he'd help hold the crowd there!

George didn't make speeches when his mother was running for Governor in 1966, because he was playing the guitar and singing at her rallies. He was at the opening rally in Montgomery, the state capital. And he played for my own rallies when I ran for President in 1968, for Governor again in 1970, and for President once more in 1972.

Having a son has given me a lot of pleasure. I had two daughters before he was born, and I *needed* a son . . . although all three of my daughters are very dear to me; I wouldn't give them up!

What do I want for George's future? Well, I want him to have the kind of future *he* wants. I just want it to be such that when he leaves this earth, he will have left it better than he found it.

I hope that whatever he does, in whatever field, he will at least *contribute* something.

If it's in the field of entertainment, then it would be the pleasure and happiness of people. And if it's not in that field, then, whatever field he's in, I hope he makes a contribution.

I think that *anybody* in our system who is successful —as a farmer, or a laboring man, or a businessman, or a professional man—is able to serve. If you're a doctor, you serve. If you're an engineer, you serve. If you're a brickmason, you serve.

But if you're just a no-'count who turns out to be a hophead, then you don't contribute anything to yourself or to your fellowman, either one.

I feel that George *will* make a contribution. And with the system under which we live, you've got to have people of talents and abilities utilizing them in order to help their fellowmen.

Some people say, "I don't *want* anything out of life! I just want to go out in the woods and lie around, do my own thing and enjoy myself, and not relate."

Well, if you just want to lie in the sun under a tree and eat fruit and sleep, that may be a pleasant life to *you*, but you're very selfish. You're not *giving* anything.

I don't know if what I say makes sense or not. But the people that claim, "I want to get out and do my own thing," they've probably got a wrist watch, and maybe an air-conditioner in their room, and perhaps an automobile. And maybe their daddy's providing all of it.

Well, it took somebody to have the intelligence to design all those things, to make them and distribute them. Everything that we enjoy, in this life in which we live, was provided by somebody's ingenuity and industry. And I think anybody that comes into the world should want to repay others for those contributions in whatever way he can.

That's been a long and roundabout way of saying I'm glad George wants to make his own contribution to the world. But as I told him the other night, "Maybe then you can pay *me* back for some of what you *cost* me!"

George, I was only joking, hear? It's been a pleasure.

THE WALLACES OF ALABAMA

Chapter One

THE SUMMER MANSION of the Governor of Alabama commands a long and beautiful strip of secluded beach on Alabama's Gulf shores. It was there that my mother, Gov. Lurleen Burns Wallace, spent her final vacation and her last carefree days in the summer of 1967, less than a year before her death from cancer.

And six years later, in the summer of 1973, that was where I nearly drowned, a hundred feet from shore.

I was twenty-one years old at the time and had recently signed a contract to sing and play for MGM Records. I had come to the Summer Mansion for the weekend with a friend of mine, Jerry Hill, a twenty-three-year-old ex-Marine who is now a singer. Jerry had brought along his wife, Donna, and their little boy, Jason.

The waves were several feet high that day, but Jerry and I are both good swimmers. And we had two small Styrofoam rafts that were just big enough to keep us afloat. So we decided it would be fun to take a swim while Donna, who had Jason with her in the house, was fixing us something to eat.

The water was even rougher than it had looked from shore, and when I was some distance out a big wave knocked my raft out of my hands and carried it away. I thought nothing of it at the time, for I had often swum far out to sea with no raft at all.

Jerry was twenty feet closer to shore than I was, but I thought I could handle the heavy surf alone. I didn't realize I was already caught in an undertow that was dragging me out to sea.

Jerry waved to make sure I was all right, and I confidently waved back to signal that I was okay.

But a few moments later I suddenly realized that I was over my head and having some difficulty swimming—because I was trying to reach the shore, but I now saw that I was being swept further and further away from it.

When I discovered that I was caught in the undertow, I anxiously scanned the water for Jerry and spotted him some distance away. I quickly motioned for him to come help me.

Jerry tried his best to reach me, but the waves were pushing him back toward the shore, while the riptide kept pulling me out to sea.

As I looked back and saw Jerry was getting further away from me than ever, I realized I was growing tired. And I began to sense at last that I was in real trouble. My legs and arms were growing weaker and weaker from their exertions.

I knew I should swim parallel to the shore to try

to escape the undertow—that was what I had always heard—and I tried that. But I couldn't seem to elude the steady tugging at my body, and I was rapidly becoming too exhausted to fight it at all.

The waves were breaking over my head now, sending me crashing down below the surface and leaving me to fight my way back up to the top, each time with more difficulty, to get some air. But I kept taking in sea water along with the air.

The struggle and the water I was swallowing and the lack of oxygen were sapping away every bit of my strength. But I kept thinking, "Don't panic . . . don't panic." And I didn't, or that would have been the end.

When I looked for Jerry again, he was still close to the shore, trying to get out to me. It didn't look like he was getting anywhere, and after that I stopped looking for him to help me.

Gradually the world around me began to blur and turn white. My eyes could no longer focus. And as I struggled to keep my head above the heavy surf and fought for air, I thought: "This is what Dad said it was like when he lay on the ground after he'd been shot—when he waited for everything to fade away and death to come."

My father, Governor George Corley Wallace, was many miles away in Montgomery. But I had never felt as close to him as I did at that moment when I thought I would never see him again.

Like everyone else, I had heard that your whole life seems to flash through your mind when you feel you're about to die. And now I learned for myself that it's really true. It was happening to *me* as I kept sinking below the surface and fighting my way back up, only to be thrown underneath once more, with the water pushing its way into my lungs.

I thought about my mother—seemed to remember *everything* about her at that moment—how good she'd always been to us, her gentle ways, the sacrifices she had made to help us, the fun we'd had together, and how lost we had all felt when she died.

As I sank below the surface into the swirling depths once more, my racing mind seemed to be detached from my weary body, which was carrying on a reflex struggle of its own to survive. My thoughts were elsewhere now.

I was thinking about Dad—the things we'd done together when I was a child, how proud I'd always been of him—and I remember suddenly thinking that it wasn't *time* for me to go yet. Because I hadn't left anything behind. I hadn't *accomplished* anything.

Dad had already done so much to help the people of our state, yet *he* had been spared from death for some purpose—to finish what he was trying to do. But I had done nothing. I *couldn't* give up and die.

The next thing I remember, I came up once more— but I knew it was getting close to the end, because I wouldn't be able to hold out much longer.

Then I looked up, and—Jerry was about ten feet away, swimming toward me with his raft. It was slowing him down, but he needed it against the undertow into which he was now swimming to rescue me.

He reached me and I grabbed one end of the raft. It was the greatest feeling I've ever had in my life when I took hold of it.

From then on, we both managed to stay above the water as we slowly made our way out of the riptide and then toward shore, with the little raft keeping us afloat. And Jerry gasped, "Man, I never thought I was gonna *get* to you!" But he had saved my life.

When we reached shore, I lay exhausted on the sand until I had a little of my strength back. My thoughts returned to that moment in the ocean when the world had seemed about to fade away, as it almost had for my father a year before.

And I felt once again my new bond of kinship with him—a bond that was stronger than any family ties— the kinship of those who have faced the seeming certainty of death and, unlike countless others but for some un- doubted reason, have come back to finish whatever in their lives remained undone.

Perhaps that is why I have never before told anyone but my father about the day I nearly drowned, in the angry waters off the Gulf shores.

Chapter Two

WHEN YOUR MOTHER has died of cancer at the age of forty-one after only sixteen months as Governor of Alabama . . . when your father, in his second term as Governor, has been shot and nearly killed in the middle of his campaign for President . . . and when you yourself have come within a few breaths of drowning at the age of twenty-one . . . well, you don't ask yourself a few weeks later whether it's too soon to start working on the story of your family, as a possible contribution to the history of our times. You only wonder how soon you can finish it and still get everything in.

With many books, this would be the spot to go back to the beginning of the story and work up to the present. First, though, I want to let you know how I feel about my father . . . to touch on a few memories that won't wait . . . to give you some idea of what you will find in this book, and to thank some of the friends and relatives who have helped me with it.

§ 8 §

Let me say here that my dad is still a fighter, and I believe that he will walk again under his own power.

But, whatever happens, he will always stand tall in my heart.

It may sound corny to say how much I love and respect my father—like coming out for God, motherhood and the American flag.

But if you're looking for cynicism, sophistication or scandal, you're reading the wrong book, because I *am* proud of my father. And I believe I can reveal what he's like inside without tearing him apart.

You have to understand that where I come from, your parents and your country and the old-fashioned "square" values are still important. One of the reasons my dad has been so successful in politics is because to many people he embodies those values and tries to speak for the average Americans who hold them.

I try to live by those values as best I can, even though I belong to a generation that also has some new values of its own, many of which I share.

But I have to be careful. I can't be as free as others of my own age. If I got into trouble in any way, it would be in headlines the next day and would reflect on my father, even though he had nothing to do with it.

And that's true of everyone in the Wallace family. People who oppose my father politically try to get at him through us. Even if no political enmity is involved, whenever someone with a famous name gets in trouble it makes news.

Being the only son of the Governor of Alabama, in my state I meet with a lot of automatic respect and attention that is really a reflection of my father's position and prestige.

But the minute I cross that Mason-Dixon line or go West, I meet a lot of hostility as well, from people who don't agree with George Wallace—even though Dad is one of the most popular politicians in the country and ranks sixth on the Gallup Poll of the world's most admired men. And some of that hostility automatically rubs off on me because of my name.

Sometimes these two strong and conflicting responses, neither of which I have really evoked by myself, are awfully hard to handle. But I still hope to win acceptance somehow on my own, while not rejecting a heritage of which I'm very proud.

In many ways I'm like any other young musician—and in many ways I'm obviously not.

Rejection of one of my performances by an audience, or the failure of a record to become a hit, can send me into a mood of deep depression, until I force myself to try again. That's common among musicians.

But when I'm invited to appear on a national television talk show, I always know I might very well not be there except for my father's fame. All I can do in such a case is politely answer the questions the host invariably asks me about my father, sing and play a song or two, and hope that people like my music once they've heard it.

I can't change my name, and I would never really want to. Because I'm proud of it and proud of my parents' achievements, and I love my family deeply.

I really miss my mother. I'm glad my father has found happiness in a new marriage, because he was so miserable after my mother died. But for me, as for most sons, *nobody* can replace my own mother. Her loss is the greatest tragedy I've ever known, and it still hurts, every day of my life.

My father, my mother, my sisters and I were always very close and loving even when we were separated by the long miles and the countless hours of his campaigns for Governor of Alabama and President of the United States.

I missed him very much when he was away, just as he missed his family. But I know now that he was doing what he believed in, carrying a message he felt must be told to the state and the nation.

When my mother died of cancer on May 7, 1968, my dad in his grief did his best to be both father and mother to my sisters and me. I'll always be grateful to him for that, just as I am proud of what he has achieved in public life.

And because of the bravery he has shown since he was shot and paralyzed from the waist down, I am prouder than ever to be his son and bear his name.

My father wants me to be an individual, and I am. This is *my* story—the story of what it is to grow up as the son of two governors, who to me have always been Mother and Dad.

But it is also the story of our family.

And in telling it I have had the help of many people, who have added their recollections to my own and allowed me to quote them extensively in this book.

My grandmother, Mozelle Wallace, recalled my father's early years for me, as did my father's brothers, Jack and Gerald, and his sister, Marianne.

My own sisters, Bobbi Jo, Peggy and Lee, have been very helpful with their reminiscences, as has my stepmother, Cornelia Wallace.

Cornelia's mother, Mrs. Ruby Austin, is one of the most colorful characters I've ever met, and she has shared her vivid memories with me. She is the sister of former

Gov. James ("Kissin' Jim") Folsom and was his official hostess when my stepmother was a little girl and they all lived in the old Governor's Mansion, which has now been torn down.

My childhood friend, Charles T. (Buddy) Weston, remembers my dad as a judge in my home town of Clayton, Alabama, and often used to visit Dad's courtroom to sit fascinated, as he held court in his own inimitable way.

Buddy also recalls my mother's many kindnesses to him and his visits to our house in Clayton, as well as our boyhood adventures.

And comedian Dave Gardner, an old friend of the family and one of my own best friends, has told me some hilarious stories about Mother and Dad that may surprise you. If you think Lurleen Wallace was a meek little woman who was completely dominated by her husband, Dave's anecdotes will change your mind!

Mrs. Jack P. Wise knew my father in college, was a close friend of my mother's, and is the mother of one of my closest friends. She comforted me when I stayed at their house while my mother was in a Texas hospital for cancer surgery and treatments during her final illness.

A member of my father's cabinet, Col. E. C. Dothard, Alabama's director of Public Safety, bought me my first guitar when I was a little boy. He has been a friend of the family since Dad was a judge—and he was shot while trying to protect my father when Dad was wounded in Laurel, Maryland, in 1972.

I have asked Colonel Dothard to tell me his memories of that day: the shooting, the immediate aftermath, and the frantic ambulance trip to the hospital in Silver Spring, Maryland, where I joined Dad and the others after flying from Alabama to be at his side.

All these people have added so much of value to this book with their vivid recollections that I owe them my deepest thanks.

This is not really a political story, although politics of course has its place in it.

It is the very human story of the private life my family has shared through the years, a story that has never been told before.

It also concerns the love, the guidance, the support and the strength each of my parents gave me. These have enabled me to live my own life as an adult whose goals happen to lie in the field of music rather than politics.

My dad, as you might expect, originally hoped I would be a lawyer. But he understands and backs my decision to seek a career in music.

He's happy that I am composing, singing and playing my own songs on MGM records now, and appearing on stage and television.

And why *shouldn't* he understand my interest in music? After all, when my dad was young he wasn't only the Golden Gloves bantamweight champion of Alabama *twice*. He was also playing guitar at square dances in his home town of Clio to make pocket money, with a fiddle player named Cass Welch, a black man who had taught Dad to play guitar for twenty-five cents a lesson.

Cass had to lean over and whisper "Change!" to my father at those dances whenever it was time to change chords.

No, my dad was never a very good guitar player. But he has always been a terrific fighter. Today he leaves the guitar playing to me, and I leave the fighting to him.

He has all kinds of courage—and not only physical courage. It took a very painful kind of emotional courage for him to go against my mother's wishes in a very private matter after she died and hope that she would have understood. I will tell you about that sad but very brave decision later—a decision I shared in.

George Wallace may not have been able to spend as much time with his family as some men do, but he made every moment with us count. And he always seemed to be there for the big moments in my life: the first day I went to school, my longest touchdown run, and the day my recording contract with MGM was announced.

So I cherish the memory of all our times together in a very special and loving way, and I always look forward to the next time I'll see him.

Today I do see my father more often than ever before—I am living in the Governor's Mansion in Montgomery now that I am a student at Huntingdon College—yet we always have a lot to talk about, and I never tire of his company.

From my earliest childhood I have always found him as fascinating as anyone would who was speaking to him for the first time. And in talking to Dad and our friends and family for this book, I have learned much about him that I never knew before.

I have wonderful memories of my mother, too, and much of this book is about her. I can still see her standing on the shore near our family cottage at Lake Martin, fishing for brim with a cane pole.

(If you don't know what brim is, you haven't been to Alabama!)

I can remember how good the brim tasted when she fried it up fresh and served it to us with hush puppies and her own homemade cole slaw.

(If you don't know what hush puppies are, you *must* come to Alabama!)

Above all, I remember her devotion to us. For instance, she used to drive to another town to do her shopping when I was very young, just so she could get a free encyclopedia volume with her grocery purchases every week for us children to have. It was the only way we could own one at the time.

I used to read to my mother from that *Little Golden Book Encyclopedia,* a column at a time, as she listened proudly.

Today the supermarkets are *selling* encyclopedias, not giving them away. But in the first volume of one of them, *Funk & Wagnalls New Encyclopedia,* is a photo of my mother and father. I only wish my mother were here to see it with me, because today *I'm* the one who's proud of *her.* But then, I always was, long before she became Governor.

I constantly tried to make *both* of my parents proud of me, and struggled to keep growing—literally! I remember how I always wanted to be taller than my older sister, Peggy. When you're a little boy, that's very important.

At the dinner table, Mother would insist that we eat enough, no matter how impatient we might be to get away and be doing something else. I was glad to oblige, because my mother was a wonderful cook. In fact, I'd take a bite, then jump up and get Peggy to stand next to me so I could see if that bite had made me taller than she was.

I was forever getting my dad to witness my latest accomplishment: "Watch me dive, Daddy!" (As he has told you!) "Watch me ride my bike, Daddy!" And even today—"Listen to my new record, Dad. What do you think of it?" I have always held him very high, and his approval still means everything to me.

Not long ago my father phoned me from Alabama

one evening while I was on a recording trip to Los Angeles. "I just want you to know that we're pulling for you, Son," he told me. He wants me to make it on my own in my chosen field.

And *I* am pulling for my dad to *walk* again on his own, for the first time since that day in May of 1972 when I feared that I had lost him forever.

Now I want to tell you the story of my family as we ourselves have lived it, and as we and our friends remember it, so that you might know us better.

I have asked my grandmother, Mozelle Wallace, to help me begin by sharing her recollections of her son, George Wallace, in the days of his youth. . . .

Chapter Three

I RECENTLY ASKED my grandmother what my father was like as a boy.

"Oh, just about like any ordinary boy," she told me. "He played football; he played baseball. He didn't care too much about fishin'. I think even when he was at *that* age he had a tendency to want to be with people. He would rather be talkin' to people than bein' home doin' work that *I* had prepared for him to do!

"He was a good student," Mozelle added. (I've always called her Mozelle, or—when I was a little boy—Mamaw, which is an old southern expression for Grandma.) "But he wasn't as good as your Uncle Jack. Jack made the dean's list when they were at the University of Alabama together. George didn't *make* the dean's list. He was out mixin' and minglin' with the students."

Even in college, Dad was an officeholder. He was president of the freshman class, a member of the Law

School Honor Court, and a member of a legal fraternity, Phi Alpha Delta.

And, Mozelle recalled, "He was president of the Spirit Committee, which made all the arrangements for homecoming."

In 1973, Dad returned to the University of Alabama to crown the Homecoming Queen, who was black. Network television cameras showed him telling her, "Congratulations! You're a mighty pretty queen."

That was quite a change from the day in 1963, also covered by national television, when he stood in a doorway at the University and barred the admission of the first black students.

Having thus signified his protest over a federal court order for their admission, which he considered to be an unconstitutional infringement on states' rights, he stood aside after the Alabama National Guard was federalized, and the students were enrolled.

Yes, Alabama has changed a lot in ten years—and so has my father. In this book you will learn just how and why, as seen from within our family. Today segregation is a thing of the past in Alabama, and George Wallace and the South as well as the rest of the country have accepted this.

But that's getting ahead of my story. We were talking about my father's childhood, and nobody can tell about that better than my Uncle Jack, who is Dad's youngest brother. He is now a circuit judge.

My father was born in Clio, a town of a few hundred people in the southeastern section of Alabama, on August 25, 1919, the son of George C. Wallace, Sr., and Mozelle Smith Wallace. His brother, Gerald, who is now a successful lawyer in Montgomery and is also my manager, was born in 1921, and Jack in 1922. So the three of them grew up together. Their only sister, Marianne, now Mrs. Alton Dauphin, is fourteen years younger than Dad—almost of a different generation.

"Although we lived right in Clio," Uncle Jack recalls, "Daddy owned two or three small farms a few miles out of town. He would furnish the land, the seeds and the fertilizer, and the tenants would furnish the labor. Then each would own half of the crop. It was share-cropping.

"We boys worked some on the farms, doing a little plowing and putting out soda around the corn, but it wasn't a day-in, day-out thing. One year we had a tenant that got in some trouble with the law and had to move off, and we had to gather that entire crop—pick the cotton and everything else.

"We had a big garden out in the back of our house, and we worked in it. Some of your beans, you know, are runnin' beans. They'd grow on vines instead of bushes, and you'd have to stick 'em. So we'd go to the woods and get tree branches, and use them to stick the beans. And we'd put some sticks by the tomato vines to hold 'em up off the ground when they'd get loaded with tomatoes. It was a lot of work.

"We'd pick the vegetables, and then we'd shell the peas and the butter beans, and your grandmother would can the vegetables in Mason jars. The housewives and mothers were busy all summer canning in those days."

The Great Depression of the early 1930s hit landlords and tenants alike, and the Wallaces were no exception. "The farming was still good, but you didn't get any price for what you'd raised," Gerald remembers.

"Cotton was eight and ten cents a pound. Today

it's eighty cents. Beef cattle—and we raised a lot of cattle—were six and eight cents a pound. It was just a struggle to *survive,* and people literally starved to death in those days.

"Everybody was poor in our section of the country during the depression. It wasn't any disgrace to be poor. There were hundreds of people who had *nothing* to do. Aside from farmers, about the only people that had jobs worked for the railroad or for the federal government, such as mail carriers. Men who worked for the county made fifty dollars a month driving a tractor or keeping the roads up. And fifty dollars a month was a big salary."

Gerald believes that's when my father became interested in helping the average man—the small farmer and the factory worker. "He just saw what was happening to the downtrodden, the people who had nothing— the people who *wanted* to work. They weren't lazy. They were all good, substantial family people with just nothing to *do.*"

Although my grandfather was a landholder, he wasn't much better off than other men. "We wore shirts our mother had made out of feed sacks," Gerald recalls.

"Everybody was in the same boat," Jack agrees. "You didn't feel left out just because you didn't have any spending money, or even any money for new clothes— because your friends didn't have any, either.

"You simply made your own entertainment, using a little ingenuity, and patched up the clothes you had. Your shoes would be half-soled several times, just as long as the tops were good.

"But we still managed to have fun. We had an uncle that had some cows, and we'd get these yearlings— little steers—and we'd break 'em to a yoke and hook 'em to a cart we'd made ourselves, using the wheels of a throwaway peanut picker. And that was our means of transportation.

"And we rode yearlings bareback, you know. We used to have one that could fight, and we'd have a pretty good time with him. But *that'll* consume a summer, just about, foolin' over some yearlings. . . .

"We made our own toys," Jack continued. "One was a kind of popgun. You see, a chinaberry tree has a little green berry that's a little hard. And we'd go down to the woods and find what they called a popgun elder. It had a pithy center that you could knock out. And that would make a barrel just like a gun barrel.

"You'd take a piece of oak and whittle it down to where you had a plunger that just fit into the barrel. You'd take the end of the plunger and hit it on the pavement and make a kind of a bushy wad on the end. That made it airtight, you see.

"You'd put one chinaberry in the barrel, and what you'd call your staff would be about an inch *shorter* than the barrel. So the chinaberry would stop an inch from the front end. Then you'd put another berry in the back and ram it home, and the air pressure would shoot that front one out. And you'd shoot it out of sight!

"So we made those things, and we'd go 'round and have popgun fights—and they wouldn't hurt you, although I guess if you got hit in the *eye* they would.

"Your daddy and I got along all right, but we fought just like all brothers do," Jack admitted. "We'd just fight about everything!

"I really think that's how George got into the boxing business, though. Daddy got us some boxing gloves just for self-protection. We'd get in a fuss, and he'd make us put the gloves on. 'Course, George kept at it and became a boxer.

"We tore our house down in 1933 and built a smaller one on the same lot in Clio—it was directly across the street from where the grocery shops and shoe shops began. We had a lot of lumber left over, and we'd use that to build clubhouses. We'd call 'em ranch houses. And, you know, *that* takes half a summer, building a clubhouse and digging your basement under it, with a trapdoor, and tunnels leading out from it. I guess that was the Tom Mix influence.

"We'd go to the picture show on Saturday. Clio's only about 800 or 900 people to this day, but we had a movie there. We started going back in the silent days.

"The man that ran the picture show was Mr. Woods Baxter. He ran an IGA store—that was the Independent Grocers Alliance—and George and Gerald and I would deliver his circulars on Saturday morning for a free pass to the movie that afternoon.

"We built a fish pond one summer, with the help of an old gray mule—a real *slow* mule that was safe enough for us to ride. Three or four of us used to ride it at one time. We took a slip pan, they called it—a device to dig dirt with—and four or five of us would hold onto the handles of it to dig the pond, because if it would take too big a bite out of the dirt it would flip and throw you over the mule.

"So we built a fish pond that way, and I think we had about two fish in it. But we'd go swimming in it. We just had a real good boyhood, because we grew up in a small town, and no danger of any violence to you, wherever you went. Your parents didn't have to worry about you all day long, wondering what trouble you were in. We had a pretty happy existence. And it didn't *take* very much money for all *that,* of course. There wasn't very much in town you could *spend* money on!

"So I'd say the difference between your generation and your daddy's generation is just a hundred percent. It's a different world now, and young people who didn't come up in the depression don't have the same outlook on life, the same values we had," Jack observed. "Not saying that you're any *worse* for it. Maybe we could profit some from *your* values. . . .

"You can't fault children for not working around the house today. What work is there to *do* around the house if you live in town? What's a teen-ager going to do now when you tell him to gather the eggs? Where's the *hen?*

"But we were born and reared in a time when people had to work and make do and just scrimp and get by on what they could. And ever since then, we've tried to live through our children, being sure that *they* got a bike even if we'd never had one. You know, Gerald bought a second-hand bike for five dollars one time, and that's the only bicycle that ever was in our *family,* back in those days.

"Parental discipline was stricter than it is today. We were switched right regularly, I would say! But I don't think we ever got one that we didn't deserve. We didn't have any real stern parents or anything like that. They just had some mischievous kids! We were getting in trouble, and sometimes they would point us in the right direction with a peach tree switch."

My dad's mother, Mozelle Wallace, thinks it was his father who pointed him in the direction of politics—but not with a peach tree switch. It happened by example, she believes.

"His daddy was in politics," Mozelle noted. "He never did run for anything himself, but he was always helping someone else in their campaign, and I think maybe that's where George got a little bit of the politics in his mind.

"George's grandfather, Dr. G. O. Wallace, at one time was a probate judge," Mozelle recalled, "and my husband was *going* to run for judge. But he wasn't able to because of his health.

"When your daddy was in high school, he was a page in the legislature at the age of fifteen. That was during the 1935 summer session—they called it the May session. And that's really when he started politics." He was elected a page by the legislators after his father took him to Montgomery to meet them and campaign for the job.

"He moved to Montgomery for the summer," Mozelle continued, "and stayed at a boardinghouse." Then she added with motherly pride, "He did *fine* as a page. Then he went back to high school in Clio."

My father was elected president of the 1937 senior class. He was also a Boys State delegate. He wasn't losing any time getting his political career going. But he found time to play quarterback for the Barbour County High School varsity football team. He won the Alabama Golden Gloves Championship as a bantamweight in 1936, and again in 1937.

If he inherited his interest in politics from his father, fortunately he did not inherit his father's health.

"Daddy had *terrible* health," Uncle Jack recalled. "He died a natural death at the age of forty!

"He had pneumonia as a baby, and one lung died," Jack explained. "He was always short of breath. And then he had sinus trouble and was operated on, and they removed some bone right at the top of his nose, between the eyebrows." The operation left a depression at the center of his forehead.

"He ended up dying with Brill's disease. It's a high fever," Jack noted. "He had such a low resistance that it just—well, knocked him out.

"His death made us become men a little quicker than we probably would have otherwise," Jack believes. "George was a freshman in college at the time. We would *still* have had to work our way through school even if Daddy hadn't died, but not as much work as we did.

"Fortunately, Mother was self-sufficient. She had majored in music in college, and had come to Clio as a music teacher. But when Daddy died, she took a job as a sewing-room supervisor for the National Youth Administration there in Clio, teaching girls how to sew and cook—how to be homemakers. That made it possible for her to support herself and Marianne, who wasn't but five or six years old when Daddy died. And that left *us* free to get out and make our own, because we didn't have to support *them*.

"Since George was already at the university when I arrived in 1939, he kind of prepared the way for me. I went to the same boardinghouse he was staying in, and he got me a job with the lady, Mrs. Sanders, that ran the boardinghouse. I worked six hours a day waiting on tables, just for my food. And then I worked two hours a day for the NYA on campus at twenty-five cents an hour. That paid your tuition. We didn't get any cash money out of it."

My father was just as busy as Jack, if not busier. Mrs. Jack P. Wise, an old friend of Dad's from Clayton, has told me just how busy he *was*.

"George was the people's idol even when he was a youngster in Clio," she remembers. "He was always political, mind you! Always politickin' and enterin' into the activities of the county.

"I didn't know him well when I lived in Clayton, but he would be pointed out in Clayton or in Louisville or Eufaula, some of the surrounding areas: 'That is George Wallace!' He was always trying to offer assistance or do whatever he could.

"I knew his grandfather, Dr. Wallace, and his grandmother, who was our postmistress in Clayton for a number of years after Dr. Wallace's death," Mrs. Wise added. "She was the most stately, erect person you've ever seen, and she was very flexible in handling the public and serving in her office. And people loved her. She was just an elegant person—had the most beautiful gray hair!

"After George got to be up in his teens, of course, he went to the University of Alabama, at Tuscaloosa," Mrs. Wise continued. "And I *lived* at the university at the time. My mother had moved there to try to get all of her eggs in one basket and get all of her children in college there.

"George was very self-sufficient. He boxed, and he took a big part in the campus activities, and he *did* for himself. And it is my understanding that with his undertakings on the University of Alabama campus he managed to educate himself. Am I correct, George?"

"Yes, Ma'm," I replied.

"He boxed, and held three or four jobs," she added. "He worked on campus for some of the deans. Am I not right, George?"

"He worked in the registrar's office. And he also waited on tables, and drove a truck and a taxi," I said.

"He had to gather coat hangers to pay for his first meal on campus."

Mrs. Wise revealed, "He worked for my sister in her place of business. She had two eating restaurants, and he did some extra work there for some meals. He supervised the help, more or less.

"George was a person who possessed an understanding of people and had *contact* with people—the public. And you could say he was a leader. He could manage the help and direct the young men that were working there. And even back in the kitchen, if anything needed to be directed about the food or anything, George could do it. And he did it with *dignity*. There was not any dissension wherever he was.

"And I will say he was a person of great fortitude," Mrs. Wise declared. "He didn't just accept what was handed to him. He *fought* for what he wanted. But he earned it in such an honest manner that he got along well with his fellowmen. He maintained quite a standard in his way of thinking, yet he was flexible and possessed great humility. He was a very humble person, and you might say that he was a very *fastidious* person.

"He was very outgoing and understanding. He never thought that he was so important on campus that he couldn't give you the time that you deserved. And even on up to this time now, he is *still* of that disposition. He has time and understanding for everyone."

As you can see from what Mrs. Wise told me, the qualities that helped my father win election as Governor of Alabama were quite fully developed by the time he reached college, leading to his success as a campus politician and laying a foundation for his later electoral successes.

And from what Mrs. Wise remembers of my father's grandmother, who was known as Mother Mae and died in 1970 at the age of eighty-eight, some of his charm may well have been inherited from her!

However, Dad's collegiate successes, which Mrs. Wise has so graciously enumerated with a charm all her own, completely failed to impress his kid sister—my Aunt Marianne. When he came home on vacations, she viewed him somewhat differently. "Fastidious" was not a word she would have used to describe him, I'm afraid.

"I just remember how proud he was of that horrible boxing picture of his! Have you seen it?" Marianne asked me recently. "It's that picture where he was boxing and his opponent was bleeding.

"To a woman it was a very *grotesque* picture!" she said with a shudder. "And he would bring it home from the university and hang it on the wall.

"He'd come home for Thanksgiving or the Christmas holidays, along with his toothbrush—and that was about it. He was clean, but he never cared for clothes. He never *had* any new clothes, because clothes just were not important to him. Neither was eating."

"Even today, he just eats to live," I agreed.

"George was very popular with everybody at the university, including the girls—he was a very nice-looking young man!" Marianne allowed. "When the boys came home from school for the holidays, George would usually bring friends with him.

"And when he came home, he liked to be out on the streets, talking to people," she added. "He could never sit still in those days. He just loved to be with *people!*"

She smiled and shook her head. "Jack would come home from school and he'd stay at home—he'd tinker around the house or do something like that. But your daddy always wanted to be out talking to people on the street about just *anything*. He was always on the go! He never could just sit. . . ."

My father received a law degree from the University of Alabama in 1942. Since the nation was at war, he enlisted in the Army Air Corps for pilot training. And while waiting for induction, he managed to obtain his first job with the State of Alabama, whose governor he would one day be. The job: driving a dump truck for the State Highway Department.

He had stayed on in Tuscaloosa after finishing college. He was twenty-three years old. One day he walked into a dime store and struck up an acquaintance with a beautiful sixteen-year-old clerk. Her name was Lurleen Burns, and they started going together. Very soon they were in love.

They were already engaged when my father received his orders to report to pilot school in Arkadelphia, Arkansas. Soon after he started his training he developed spinal meningitis and nearly died.

"He had one of the worst cases," Mozelle recalls. "He was unconscious for six days. But they let him come home on convalescent leave when he was physically able to make the trip. And that's when he married Lurleen.

"I *liked* Lurleen. She was a mighty sweet person to me. But I never was able to *be* with them too much, because I was working." When Marianne was in the fourth grade, Mozelle took her to Montgomery and went to work for the State of Alabama after selling the house and farms my grandfather had owned.

"I was secretary to the director of the Bureau of Preventable Diseases for twenty-five years," Mozelle remembers with justifiable pride. Never did she have to depend on her children for help of any kind, a matter of great personal satisfaction to her. She is now retired.

When my father was well enough to return to active duty in the Air Corps, my mother went with him and lived near the base in Arkansas, and then followed him from duty station to duty station.

She returned to her parents' home in Mobile, Alabama, to give birth to Bobbi Jo in 1944. Then she rejoined Dad in Alamogordo, New Mexico, where they lived in a converted chicken house for a time with their baby. When Dad was sent overseas, my mother went back to Alabama with Bobbi Jo to await his return.

His serious illness had knocked my father out of pilot training. He fought in the Pacific as a flight engineer on a B-29 nicknamed The Sentimental Journey, bombing the coast of Japan from a base in the Marianas.

The noise of the aircraft engines during these flights left him with permanently impaired hearing, although he stubbornly refused to wear a hearing aid until just a couple of years ago. It's in his proud nature to yield as little as possible to *any* physical impediment, as the whole nation has recently learned.

After the war, my parents settled in Clayton, a few miles from Clio, and Gov. Chauncy Sparks appointed my father an assistant attorney general. But Dad soon took a leave of absence to run for the Alabama House of Representatives in the fall of 1946, and won. He was only twenty-seven when he was elected to the legislature on the Democratic ticket.

Mozelle admitted to me, "I've never cared too much for politics. But when George told me he was going to run, I said, 'If that's what you want to do, just go ahead and do it!' Because I felt he was old enough to *know* what he wanted to do. And if a political life was what he wanted to lead, it was up to George to venture out in it.

"Naturally I worried about him when he was campaigning. I think running for *any* political office is hard on a person.

"But George has been mighty good to me," Mozelle said. "I have no complaint about *any* of my children. I'm so independent myself that they don't know what to do for me, but if I needed anything they would be right there."

While my father was in the Alabama legislature, he was considered something of a radical because he favored the common people against the Establishment. But he was twice voted one of the outstanding members of the legislature for sponsoring acts that brought county and municipal employees under Social Security, created junior colleges and trade schools, increased job opportunities in industry, and provided free tuition for widows and children of war casualties.

Meanwhile, Dad's brother Gerald was suffering from a serious case of tuberculosis contracted during his military service in the South Pacific. His case didn't respond to medication, and finally he had to have part of a lung removed. Gerald's illness, which kept him an invalid for ten years, gave rise to my father's interest and involvement in improving the care of TB patients in Alabama.

"Immediately after World War II," Gerald remembers, "veterans' hospitals were brimming over with casualties. Even TB patients had to go on a waiting list. So I was in a county hospital, waiting to get into a veterans' hospital. And that's where George learned of the low amount of money spent per day per patient in county hospitals.

"I think tubercular patients got ninety-four cents a day for care. And as a result of visiting me in the county hospital he proposed legislation, which passed, to increase their daily budget to something like $2.25 a day, which made a big difference.

"Conditions were *horrible* at the time I went into the county hospital. There were eight and ten patients crowded into each ward, and the patients had to look after the other patients, since there was not enough care. Many patients died while they were in the ward with the others, because they couldn't remove them to what was called the terminal room.

"George's interest in helping TB patients, which came about when he learned of their problems through my illness, started him on the road to helping others who were sick, infirm, or blind," Gerald told me. "His personal insight into conditions in state and county hospitals influenced him as a legislator, and later as Governor, to work toward increasing facilities and benefits for all these classes of people.

"I don't think he ever *told* me he was going to help improve conditions for patients," Gerald added. "He just *did* it."

My sister Peggy and I were born in Clayton while Dad was in the legislature. Peggy was born in 1950. And I arrived on October 17, 1951.

Or, as my mother put it when Dad took his first look at me in the hospital: "George, I've got you a son!"

Chapter Four

MY FATHER sat on a long park bench in the Clayton town square on a glittering Saturday afternoon, shirt-sleeved in the humid Alabama sunshine, and surrounded by people. It was Saturday—market day—and all the farmers from the neighboring areas of Barbour County had come to town to buy their supplies at the stores that lined the square. Many of them had drifted over to visit with my dad, whom they all knew, while I sat by him or scampered off to scale the town's Confederate monument, a weary soldier slouched forever against his silent gun.

I was five years old at the time, and Dad was Circuit Judge of Alabama's Third Judicial District, which covered Barbour, Bullock and Dale counties. He had been elected to the office in 1952.

The venerable brick courthouse, whose halls and chambers were paneled with dark and ancient woods, was deserted for the day. But it loomed impressively over the square and my father's informal deliberations.

The talk, of course, was largely of politics, and most of it was incomprehensible to me. But that didn't matter. I really enjoyed being with my dad, and looked forward to those Saturday afternoons in the town square, even though we exchanged few words.

He seemed to give off an energy and a warmth of personality that spoke their own clear message to everyone near him, myself included. Whenever he did talk to me, it was with kindness and a casual camaraderie that bridged the generations.

I already realized that my father was very popular with the citizens of Barbour County. Not only did he attract eager crowds to his bench in front of the courthouse, but whenever he strolled around town people would stop him to talk, and he was always glad to oblige. Some called him George and others called him Judge, and he knew everyone's first name.

Even though I was very young, I was welcome to visit Dad's office in the courthouse and sit behind his desk, which was always stocked with a large supply of the cigars he loved to smoke. I remember being impressed by all the lawbooks that lined the walls of the high-ceilinged old room with its lazy overhead fans.

We lived a few blocks away from the courthouse in a big white house on the corner of Eufaula and College streets. Clayton High School, which ran from grades one through twelve, was just behind our house, and from my earliest childhood I used to go there to swing and play in the schoolyard with my sister, Peggy.

"We would go up there and seesaw," Peggy recalls. "Every time I think of that playground it reminds me of *To Kill a Mockingbird*—the part where the little boy and little girl got attacked in the playground and somebody saved them."

No such threats marred our childhood, however. The first fear I can recall involved going to kindergarten for the first time when I was five. It was located in the home of a genteel elderly lady some three blocks away. I remember walking there that first day accompanied by my dad and my mother.

You had to have your own little chair, and Daddy had gone out and bought me a chair which he carried as we walked.

The proprietor of the kindergarten turned out to be very kindly, and I found that I enjoyed going to school. But above all I loved the home I shared with my father, my mother and my two older sisters. There was a warm, affectionate atmosphere there that I'll never forget.

The house had a big front porch with square pillars and was set in a large yard. A wide hallway ran through the house from front to back, and all the rooms were large, with modest but comfortable furniture: the living room, dining room, den and three bedrooms, with another dining room inside the roomy kitchen. It was hard for one person to keep up such a large house, and there was a black woman who came in and helped Mother.

But Mother spent a lot of time on the house, cleaning it and fixing it up. She remodeled the living room and a couple of the bedrooms. She was just a tremendous mother, and always wanted things to be as nice as possible for us, for she loved us all dearly.

Even outside the home, she was a very compassionate person who liked and got along well with everybody. She was reserved to a certain degree when we lived in Clayton, but when she would meet you, she was really *glad* to meet you. And you could tell that just by looking at her, because she was honest through and through.

I think when she ran for Governor of Alabama in 1966, that's what so many people saw—that honesty and that goodness. Even if they had already decided, "Well, I'm going to vote for her because I'm for George Wallace," they were twice as enthusiastic when they met her.

She loved the sunshine, loved being outdoors, and before we had a clothes dryer she really used to enjoy hanging the washing out on a clothesline in the backyard.

Often she would wander over to the high school in the morning and sip coffee with Mary Jo Ventress, a good friend of hers who taught home economics there. Mary Jo was also one of her favorite fishing companions. I can't remember Daddy ever going fishing with her, except maybe once.

The family's sole source of transportation at that time was a very old, badly faded green Chevrolet. Mother used to drive Dad to work at the courthouse and then bring the car back to use for shopping and other errands. There was a space in front of the rear window that was my particular domain, and I'd curl up there when we went for drives.

I remember how excited my mother was when Dad traded the Chevrolet in on a new brown-and-white model around 1958. She'd been wanting a new car for a long time, and he was able to use it for campaigning, an activity that had helped wear out the old green Chevy.

Since Peggy Sue and I were only two years apart in age while Bobbi Jo was several years older, Bobbi would be called on to referee our arguments. Peggy still recalls one time that I won, with some help from Mother.

"When I was six years old in 1956, I had hepatitis," Peggy reminds me. "And I had to stay flat on my back for six weeks. So my Grandmother Burns gave me a whole box of presents, just little things like coloring books, and I could open one a day.

"And I'll never forget, George, you got so jealous because you didn't have anything, so Mother let *you* open gifts, too. And I got so mad, because they were my presents and I was sick. But you sure did get to have some of them!"

Bobbi Jo, like Mother, was pretty and kind. An attractive brunette, she was very popular in high school. She has warm memories of our mother:

"The high school had some sort of contest that I was in, and you had to wear an evening gown for it. And Mother did not particularly care for sewing, but she made the dress that I wore. She made it at the high school with the help of Mary Jo Ventress, who was my home economics teacher. I remember it very well. It was turquoise, with a chiffon skirt; the top was made out of taffeta and was covered with little flower petals of the same material. I was awfully proud of the dress, because it was something that my mother had made for me, and I kept it for a long time.

"I don't like to sew, either," Bobbi Jo added, "and I'm not sure that I would sit down and get into something as involved as sewing with chiffon and taffeta. It's very difficult, and I'm sure that making that dress was a real sacrifice for Mother. But I really loved the dress."

I always liked going to school, from kindergarten

on. After mastering some of the complexities of adding, spelling and writing, I was considered ready for first grade, which occasioned another attack of nerves, even though I was again accompanied by my parents on the first day of school. But I soon started enjoying myself again, being particularly fond of arithmetic, and had good grades throughout my school years.

Although I was a well-behaved child, there were exceptions. I can remember I broke my dad's wristwatch when I was six years old. I wasn't supposed to touch it ever, but I used to get it off the chest in his bedroom and play with it. And he used to take it from me and tell me to leave it alone.

One day Dad and Mother were in the kitchen when I walked in holding the watch—and I promptly dropped it on the floor, shattering the crystal.

Dad gave me a spanking, and I cried a lot, because he'd never done that to me before. But I never played with his watch again.

My mother never did spank me—even though I ran away from home once. I must have been six or seven, and I can't remember why, but I packed my little suitcase and left the house.

I do remember that my mother helped me pack my bag—and then discreetly followed me down the street, keeping a block or so behind me.

I didn't look back for about three blocks, and that's when I saw her patiently trailing me. Soon I decided that I didn't *really* want to run away, and the whole idea started to seem a bit scary. So I walked back to where my mother was and we went home together.

Despite my minor misdeeds, we were well-disciplined children who were taught to have good manners. We always said, "Yes, Sir," "Yes, Ma'm," "No, Sir," and "No, Ma'm."

We grew up in a very religious home. We went to the First Methodist Church in Clayton, attending both Sunday School and church service.

My mother was always with us. Often, as he started touring the state in preparation for running for Governor, Dad was out of town. But both my parents were active in church activities. And when Dad was home, he went with us, and he led the singing in the church—hymns and old gospel songs. It was amusing, because my dad really couldn't sing.

He could carry a tune, but he just wasn't too good. And unfortunately he sang very loudly.

Life in a small country town in Alabama—a town like Clayton—is really peaceful, and everybody knows everybody. I remember I always looked forward to the summers because there was a community swimming pool. You paid a quarter to get in, and it was within walking distance of our house, as was almost everything in Clayton. I went nearly every day after my mother taught me to swim when I was five or six.

Sometimes Dad would go to the pool with me, but very seldom. Usually Mother and I went with Peggy. My only mishap there occurred one day when I was racing a friend named Ben Martin, and I swallowed too much water. I was pulled out coughing by the lifeguard while Mother watched worriedly. But after a few minutes of getting my breath I was all right.

When Dad went to the pool, he seldom went in swimming with us. But when I'd say "Watch me dive!" he always obliged.

"That's great!" he'd say—and then he'd resume

talking with the other fathers. Thinking back, I can see how politically ambitious he was even then. But I don't think a son could admire a father more than I do him, really, and I always did.

All my life I've wanted to prove myself to my dad because he's so strong. I remember when I had my first bicycle. It had trainers on it, and as soon as I had the trainers off and could ride it a few feet, I would get Daddy to come out in front of the house and watch me. And sometimes he helped me balance the bike as I rode along the sidewalk.

I fell a lot until I got the hang of it, but I never cried. I'd get right up and try it again. I always wanted to ride well when my dad was watching, so that he would be proud of me for knowing how to ride a bike. I was sure that would impress him.

Not only did he and I get along really well; in my eyes, my dad could do anything. I remember when I was just starting to play baseball, a group of men in the town got a couple of softball teams together and played each other. One day when I was watching him play, my dad got the only hit in the game. And as he slid into second base, one of his fingers came out of joint and he had to pull it back in. I was very proud of him.

He used to pitch a baseball to me in our yard, although he didn't do it as much as I would have liked. His career at that point was very important to him, I'm sure, and he was always traveling and trying to meet as many people as he could.

Of course, I can understand that now. But looking back, I remember that he was very *busy* all the time when I was a child—always on the go. And sometimes I would wonder why he couldn't spend any more time with *me*, or at least stay home more. I used to nag him about coming out and playing more with me.

And he would do it sometimes when I asked him, but his mind was on his career.

I remember we also used to play football in the yard. A group of my friends—and there were several black guys among them—would come and play there. And Dad would come out sometimes and throw the football.

Even though such moments together were rare because of his busy schedule, I look back on them now as among the highlights of my childhood—happy times I'll never forget.

And yet I can't recall my dad ever explaining why he couldn't spend more time with me. Because of his frequent absences, I think I relied more on my mother for company. She and I were very close. I believe she tried to fill the gap that was caused by his being gone so much. We spent a lot of time together.

My Aunt Marianne's husband, Alton Dauphin, works in my father's national campaign, and Aunt Marianne notes that men in politics "do have to be gone a lot. But you just accept it. Luckily for me, my children are older than Lurleen's were at that time. I think she probably had more influence on your lives because she was *with* you more than your daddy as you were growing up. Because he was gone so much, and I find how much they *have* to be gone since my husband has been in the campaign.

"George and Lurleen began their marriage with him campaigning," Marianne notes. "I think she took it very *well*. I'm sure it was hard on her, because she had three small children to raise almost *alone*. When my children were small and I couldn't get out of the house and my husband was away, it was a very depressing thing. I really dreaded his going."

But I never heard Mother complain about my father's increasing absences from home. It was not in her nature to reveal such feelings, but the loneliness must have been there.

Mother found a lot of joy in music, and gave me piano lessons at an early age before sending me off to a piano teacher. It could be that I acquired my own love of music from her, though I may have inherited it from both sides of the family. My grandmother, Mozelle Wallace, taught piano before marrying my grandfather.

Mother liked to bring music into everything. We would all sing in the car when we used to go visit my grandparents, Harry and Estelle Burns, on their farm in Greene County, which was about 150 miles away. I remember one of her favorites was *The Old Rugged Cross*. She *loved* to sing that. And we'd sing carols, whatever the season.

We used to go to the farm every summer for a couple of weeks, and I always looked forward to that. I liked to go hunting with my grandfather, shooting squirrels in the woods behind the pasture.

Christmas at our house was just beautiful. Mother would get really excited about it, and she always liked to start preparing as soon as possible, because she loved Christmas.

We always had a real tree, and I can remember a couple of times Dad took us out in the country to get our own tree. That made it a lot more exciting for us. And we always looked forward to decorating it.

Mother spent a lot of effort getting ready for Christmas. I can remember she would always know what you wanted for a present, even if you hadn't specifically asked for it. You might have mentioned something very casually, but she would always make a mental note of it.

And you'd always be so surprised on Christmas morning, because she'd always have chosen something that you really wanted but didn't think you could get. She would make sure you had it! That was how I got my bicycle.

On Christmas Day we'd all get up at 5:30 in the morning—except for my father, who lounged around in bed until 7:30 or 8. Every time we'd open a present, we'd run in to see him and say, "Look at this! Look at this!" Of course, *he* knew what it was before *we* knew. And eventually he'd get up and join us.

But Mother was up early, because she always liked to see our expressions when we opened our gifts and take pictures of us. In fact, she had stayed up most of the night getting everything ready and putting our presents under the tree. She'd always have them hidden.

We were all too excited to eat breakfast, but our mother would always cook a large Christmas dinner. And our relatives were invited, including my grandparents, my uncles and aunts, and my cousins.

My mother was an excellent cook. For dinner we had turkey and dressing, mashed potatoes, peas, and (sweet) potato pie, plus coconut pie, a special favorite of mine.

Afterward we would all sing carols, which my mother loved so dearly.

All in all, Christmas Day at the George Wallace house in Clayton was just a happy country Christmas, which to me is one of the most beautiful things in the world—and one of my fondest memories.

Chapter Five

BUDDY WESTON, who is now a program coordinator for Goodwill Industries in Montgomery, was one of my best friends when I was a child in Clayton, although he was five years older, and we recently reminisced about those days.

"My father had a small service station," he recalls, "and because of that I became very close to your mother. She came down to the station a lot and I used to go out and put gas in her car.

"She was a real friendly individual and took up a lot of her time with the children there in Clayton. I was only eight or nine years old when I first knew her.

"She would ask me, 'How are you today? What are you doing in school? How are your grades? You know, you've really got to have good grades if you ever expect to excel in the world.' I'd see her almost every other day.

"I never saw your father very much at first because he was always concerned with courthouse activities and things of that nature.

"I know your mother did a lot of church work with the younger children, teaching them in Sunday School. Of course, she was a Methodist and we were Baptists, but I recall she took a lot of time with the Young Methodist Fellowship.

"And then one day she came by and said, 'Why don't you come up and play with little George sometimes? He's a lot younger than you are.' I only lived four or five houses down the street from you. So I went up to your house one day, and you were building a model airplane. And you were having a helluva time—couldn't get the thing together—so I started building on it. And I ended up putting it together for you.

"And so from that time we sort of fooled around together. And then we got into the electronics phase. Remember? Portable radios were coming out real big at that time, and I had this little kit that I ordered and put together. It was a wireless transmitter where you could broadcast your voice over almost a mile area there in Clayton. So you became my disc jockey."

That was my first venture into "show business," and talking to Buddy brought it all back.

"We had it fixed up where you could play records and say things over the radio," he recalled. "We had no FCC license—nothing like that! But there was another guy in Clayton who got a transmitter, too, so we were in competition with each other. A lot of people in Clayton listened to us for a while.

"While you were my disc jockey, I remember I started going to school dances and tried to demonstrate some of the steps for you—mostly jumping around," Buddy told me. "Then a dancing teacher from Eufaula came over to Clayton and had dancing classes. You and

Peggy Sue and I went to her classes at Clayton High School a couple times a week.

"She had classes in several towns, and they all got together for a final fling where they gave out trophies for the best dancers. And I didn't get the best trophy. Neither did you. But you got the same size trophy I got—you danced the jitterbug with Peggy Sue—and I remember you carried that trophy to school for a week with your books!

"Another time, I had a model airplane with a gasoline engine, and you wanted one. So you had me stay after your daddy to get you one. I don't know how long I had to spend demonstrating to your daddy how it operated.

"Meanwhile I kept telling you, 'I don't think you can fly the thing! You're gonna tear it up!' I didn't have any confidence in you whatsoever.

"But your father bought you one just like mine—same color and same size, about a two-foot wing span. And you and he got out and flew it. The first time, it flew real good.

"And you were doing beautiful—but you had to hold onto it with a wire and follow it around, and you got dizzy and fell. And the thing crashed and was wrecked."

Buddy was one of the boys who played football and baseball in our front yard. "After a game Miss Lurleen would fix us all some sandwiches and milk," he remembers. "She always had plenty for everybody."

One day Buddy, his baseball cap on, followed me into the large center hall of our house and had the shock of his life. As he sat there waiting for me to come out of my room, he happened to glance through the open door of Bobbi Jo's room, which was next to mine. She was unaware of his presence. "Bobbi Jo was dressing, and she didn't have any clothes on," he remembers. "I was pulling my cap down over my face!"

Buddy admired Mother tremendously. "I remember one time my mother and I were buying groceries at the same time as your mother, and they gave us one of y'all's sacks and her one of ours. And Miss Lurleen walked all the way to our house with our sack and said, 'We've got y'all's groceries.' She could have phoned and I could have run over for them, but she came before we even got the groceries out."

Buddy also became good friends with my father. "I used to talk to him a lot downtown, when he sat on that bench in front of the courthouse with fifteen or twenty people around him," he remembers, confirming my own memories of those days.

"And of course Billy Watson would be there," Buddy added. Billy Watson was an older man of sixty-five or seventy who was wise in the ways of Barbour County politics and even state politics. My father was more or less his protégé and learned a lot from him over the years. Billy died a few years ago, having seen Dad become Governor. I remember hearing that when Dad and his brothers were young men and wore underwear made of feed sacks, Billy told Dad, "Stick with me, George, and you'll be wearing *silk* underwear!"

"Billy Watson was a very outspoken person," Buddy remembers. "If I looked dirty when I walked downtown, he'd say, 'Go on and tell your daddy to put you on a clean shirt. And *then* come back and talk to me.'

"Billy was very, very close to Governor Wallace in those days, always advising him. I expect he knew a lot of politics before Governor Wallace ever got started.

"But your dad would talk to people about whatever concerned them—not just politics. When he was sitting out there with the farmers, he'd talk about farming," Buddy recalls.

"And he would take up a lot of time with me. He always had a cigar in the right side of his mouth. He'd talk about just anything that I wanted to talk about, really. School, for one thing: 'What are you doing in school? You-all still making those model airplanes?' No other adults were that interested in me except my father and mother.

"There were only five or six people in Clayton that I would let help me cross the street when I was seven or eight, and Governor Wallace was one of them," Buddy told me. "It was a big trip to cross the square to the court-house—you had to go across two streets!

"He got onto me a couple of times when I'd ride my bicycle too fast downtown," Buddy added. "I'd be on the sidewalk. He stopped me one time and told me to slow down, 'because you could hurt somebody. And if you hurt somebody, you really would be sorry.' But his tone was very soft and pleasant when he said it.

"I remember I used to visit his courtroom when he was presiding. Usually the cases weren't very important. Just somebody'd be arguing over bird dogs or something like that.

"I had to go up these huge stairs to reach the courtroom—I could hardly touch the hand rail, it was so high. And the courtroom was hot, *very* hot, with just those big old overhead fans running. Governor Wallace was the type that would come out of his coat. I never *did* see him with a robe on.

"But he was a strict judge, it seemed to me; he went strictly by what it said in the book, as far as I could tell. 'Course, I didn't know the law, but he seemed to me to be very wise in his decisions.

"Sitting up there, he really had the mark of authority. And he was outspoken. If somebody told him, 'You're wrong,' he'd say, 'No, I'm not! I'm *not* wrong. I'll tell you why.' He was just that type of a person.

"They had a couple of lawyers down in Clayton who were not very good lawyers," Buddy recalled. "I mean, they weren't the dynamic type. They talked very slowly. And I could detect some amount of boredom on your dad's part at having to put up with them. Governor Wallace was the type who had to keep it moving." And Buddy snapped his fingers.

"But he was also the kind of guy who could be the judge this morning, and if you needed some advice on your farm in the afternoon, he'd be there to help you.

"Many times, if he was asked, he would go out to a man's farm if the fellow was having trouble financially with his crops. The farmer would ask him, 'Can you show me legally how I can borrow some more money?' or something like that. And your dad would take the time to advise him."

Such personal attention to everyone's interests and needs in the counties he served as circuit judge, plus his past service to the people as a state legislator, won my father a host of admirers, as did his frequent speech-making forays around the state. So the day finally came when he felt ready to enter the 1958 primary for Governor of Alabama. (The real gubernatorial contest in Alabama, for all practical purposes, is in the spring Democratic primary, not in the November general election, which is traditionally won by the Democrat.)

I can remember the day Dad came home and told us he was going to run for Governor. He walked into the den and met Mother, and when he told her the news she became very excited. I knew that it was something big, but I really couldn't comprehend what it was all about. I was only six years old.

Peggy was unimpressed. "Mother was all excited and Daddy was all nervous," as she recalls it. "He's never been a very emotional person. I don't remember Daddy *ever* getting excited—just nervous!

"I asked, 'What's going on?' And Mother said, 'Your daddy's going to run for Governor.' I didn't know what it was, either, so I just shrugged and said, 'Mmm.' So we just kind of blew with the wind on that one."

There were many candidates for Governor in the 1958 Democratic primary, but the favorites were my father and John Patterson. Patterson's father had been shot to death in Phenix City four years earlier, after winning the Democratic primary election for attorney general by promising to clean up the town, which was then very corrupt. Patterson was named to replace his father as Attorney General, and the assassination was still well remembered in Alabama in 1958.

Patterson, like my father at the time, was a segregationist. But Patterson had accepted the endorsement of the Ku Klux Klan, while my father had publicly denounced the Klan.

Of course, all I knew at the time was that my dad was running for Governor—and that was enough for me. I used to go around and hand out little campaign cards for "Judge George Wallace."

And, as he has noted, I also spoke for him. I had a memorized speech that was a page-and-a-half long. And I'd travel around with a man in a truck, giving my speech in one town while my father was speaking in another.

As Dad has pointed out, when I would speak on

the same platform with the candidates for various offices, they would hold me for last because people had heard of me and would come just to see me. I used to break up the place with my speech. So the crowd would wait for me and have to listen to the other speeches first.

I would stand up on a chair in my little navy blue suit with a white shirt and black clip-on tie, with my hair combed straight back. At that age, you know, regardless of who you are, you're cute if you're up there making a speech.

I never forgot any of the speech or had any trouble with it, and it always seemed to come off well. I had no stage fright. I really *believed* what I was saying. I remember the last line was, "With God's help, my daddy will make you a good Governor."

One time I fell asleep on the stage because I was tired. I'd been traveling all day and then I had to sit up in front of all those people while the others made their speeches. I didn't mean to go to sleep, but I was just exhausted, so I leaned back and dozed off. And they had to wake me up when it was my turn to speak.

But I really enjoyed giving those speeches. I liked meeting people, and everyone made over me. They'd say, "Well, aren't you cute? You're going to be Governor one day, aren't you?"

John Patterson led my father by 34,000 votes in the first primary, and the two went into a runoff election which Patterson won by nearly 65,000 votes. He went on to become Governor.

I remember being at Dad's campaign headquarters at the Jefferson Davis Hotel in Montgomery the night he lost the runoff. I really couldn't understand what was going on. But I could see that everyone seemed very unhappy, and some people were crying. It had been a hard campaign for everyone concerned, and it had taken a lot out of everybody. Finally I realized that Dad had lost.

There was considerable talk that night that Patterson had received a sympathy vote because of his father's murder. I'm sure there *was* some of that, but he was a good Governor and has since become a good friend of ours.

As for my father's reaction to his defeat—he's a good loser, as well as a good winner. He was going around the room cheering people up, and he was smiling. I remember that, because *I* felt so bad, and so did a lot of other people, and he seemed to stand out. Mother took his loss very well, too, and she joined Dad in comforting his campaign workers that night.

But Dad was totally exhausted after that campaign, and of course very disappointed that he'd lost. He rested for a couple of weeks, getting his strength back, and wrote thank-you notes to his supporters.

He had only a few weeks left as circuit judge, because he had not been able to run for reelection to that office since he was running for Governor. He was succeeded by his brother Jack, who had been elected in his place when Dad decided not to go after another six-year term.

"He was a good judge," Jack told me. "I practiced in his court some, and he practiced in mine after I took over. He was understanding and compassionate, and— George has got just a lot of common sense.

"He knew more law than a lot of people would think, because George was primarily a politician, not a bookworm. But actually when I took over, I took his notebook over. He got out and had other judges help him, and he compiled a three-to-four-hundred-page notebook of things that are helpful to a judge on the bench. I was real pleased to get it, because it was real good, and I've used it and I've let other judges Thermofax it entirely. They all like it."

So when Buddy Weston declared that my father "went by the book," he was perfectly right. But he must have missed out on some good cases when he thought most of them didn't amount to much. "We try everything," Jack told me, "including murders, robbery, rapes, divorces and everything else. This is our highest trial court."

When Dad's term as circuit judge ran out, he entered private law practice in partnership with his brother Gerald. Dad had a law office in Clayton, while Gerald practiced in Montgomery.

He had a small office in a new building across from the Clayton hardware store. And I remember going down there with him. His desk was always very jumbled up—papers just everywhere. But *he* knew where everything was.

Peggy Sue and I both enjoyed visiting his office. "You just don't pop into a lawyer's office in the afternoon unexpected," she notes, "but *we* always did." And Dad didn't seem to mind.

Actually, he didn't practice much law. He was soon traveling around the state again, giving speeches and meeting people, getting ready to run for Governor in 1962. Rather than being withdrawn after his defeat, he seemed, if anything, a little more energetic.

Even though he had lost the election, he had become

well-known across the state as a result of his candidacy. And he was really on the move, campaigning almost constantly.

How did my mother feel about exchanging the life of a judge's wife for that of a perennial candidate for Governor? After all, within the space of a few years everything had changed. Our father would be out of town for days on end, and Mother would be left alone with us.

I recently discussed this with a good friend of Mother's, Juanita (Mrs. C. F.) Halstead, who first met her just at the time my father was first planning to run for Governor, in 1957. They met in Montgomery, where the Halsteads live, and remained close friends until my mother's death.

"Maybe when I first met Lurleen she was not *too* keen on it, but she realized that this was what *he* wanted," Mrs. Halstead told me. "And like most wives that I know, what he wanted is what *she* wanted. And she jumped right in."

Like my father, I was optimistic about 1962. Shortly after he lost the 1958 election, I was in Montgomery with my family and we passed the big white Governor's Mansion with its imposing columns and spacious grounds. And I remember thinking to myself, "Well, that's where we would have lived if he'd won." And then I vowed, "We *will* live there one day!"

Meanwhile, there was plenty to keep me busy in Clayton. I liked school, enjoyed practicing piano, which I studied for two years, and continued my interest in sports. Some of the boys teased me about my piano lessons, but that never bothered me, because I was as athletic as any of them.

I can remember helping out the Clayton High School

§ 54 §

football team from the time I was in the second grade. I was a waterboy, really, making myself useful in any way I could. I traveled with the team when it went out of town, and I was at practice every day.

My dad and other men of the community would drive the players home after practice, because some of the players lived several miles out of town and the school buses would already have left.

I remember one particular night when my father carried three of the football players home and I went with them. I was at the age when I really looked up to football players. They were my heroes.

In the car, my dad was talking about the time when *he* was in high school and how he'd played football—and these guys didn't seem too interested! They listened, but I could tell by their expressions that they just didn't seem to care. And I couldn't understand that. Because to *me,* hearing my dad tell it was the most exciting thing in the world! And their attitude really stood out in my mind. For at that point I felt that anything my father did was fantastic.

In fact, I'm *still* proud of his football exploits—particularly one that has become a family legend.

He was a 120-pound quarterback on the high school football team in Clio, and it was a very small team. During his senior year, they played a big game against Troy, which was a much larger town. And there was really no way Clio could even compete with Troy, because Troy had more boys to pick from and the quality of the players was naturally much higher.

But Dad wrote a letter to his team and read it to them just before the game, telling them it was from Troy. The letter put Clio down in a bad way, saying, "There's no way that you-all should even *compete* with us on the field, because we're going to run over you."

And Dad really lifted the team's spirits with this challenge. The coach realized this was what he was doing as he listened to Dad reading the letter.

Troy still beat Clio, but they only beat them 6 to 0, whereas they should have whipped them by 40 to 0.

And so even at that age, my father was a fighter who never gave up. And when he lost the Governorship in 1958, it's not surprising that he considered it merely a prelude to 1962.

Chapter Six

IN 1961 my happy years in Clayton came to an end. We moved from our beautiful, spacious home to a small upstairs two-bedroom apartment in Montgomery. It was located in a low-rent apartment complex.

The reason for the move was my father's desire to be closer to the center of the campaign action, and that was in the state capital. He felt it would help him in running for Governor.

I was homesick and lonely. I didn't know a soul in Montgomery, and I felt lost in a city of 200,000 people after spending my childhood in a small town where everybody knew each other.

I enrolled in the fourth grade at Bellingrath School. The first day I walked into class, I was very nervous. The teacher introduced me to the class, and some of them knew who my father was.

That had a definite impact on me—an unfavorable one. It wasn't that I was sorry to be George Wallace's son, of course, but for the first time I was being identified with a name rather than as a person.

Some of the students were for my father, and others were against him. But that wasn't the point. I wanted to be accepted for myself as I always had been in Clayton. As a result of my classmates' attitude, I was quite shy for a while.

There was something else I wasn't even conscious of, until Peggy Sue told me about it recently. "When you were little, you had a minor speech impediment," she said. This was news to me. "It wasn't a lisp, but you couldn't pronounce certain sounds well.

"And I'll never forget—when we lived in the low-rent apartment complex in Montgomery, Oral Roberts had that TV show where he healed people. That was the big thing to watch, and they said you could send your letters in if you had a friend or a member of your family who needed healing.

"So I wrote a letter to Oral Roberts asking him to heal my little brother's speech impediment. And I never did tell anybody in the family about it until now.

"I've since had several speech courses, and I now know that your impediment was something most children grow out of. And after a few years you did grow out of it.

"Of course," Peggy noted, "now the family knows Oral Roberts personally, and he's been to the Mansion. But I've never even mentioned it to *him*."

Eventually I began to make friends in Montgomery. And after a year we moved out of our cramped apartment into an attractive three-bedroom house that we rented from a retired general who was living in another county.

We needed the extra space, for my sister Lee was born in April, 1961, just before we moved to Montgomery.

My dad called home from the hospital to tell us of Lee's birth. I had been hoping for a brother, but when they brought her home I took to her instantly, even though it scared me at first to hold her, because I'd never held a baby before.

By the time the 1962 campaign warmed up the following year, Lee was just walking. So when Dad would finish a speech, Lee would toddle out on the stage and walk to him as he stood at the podium. She would always get a big hand from the crowd.

I spoke for my father on a few occasions in 1962, but not like in 1958, for I was busy in school. Mainly I talked in elementary school classrooms and assemblies. The idea was for the kids to go home and tell their parents about my talk. I didn't have any prepared speech that year. Mainly I told the students to ask their folks to vote for my dad.

Once my mother and I spoke to a school assembly near Seneca, Alabama. And I remember on several occasions the whole family would be onstage at a rally and Dad would introduce us.

I played Little League baseball and Peewee football in 1962, on teams sponsored by a firm called Arrow Rents. And I remember that when I was campaigning for Dad that spring, I used to report late to baseball practice. One day I almost missed a game.

I was returning with some people from a campaign appearance, and they ran a lot of red lights to get me to the ball field. (Actually they'd check to see that no cars were coming, then ease on through.)

I got there halfway through the game, and just had time to get on my uniform and play the final innings.

In 1958 I had been a little young to comprehend what was happening. But I think moving to Montgomery helped me realize how important running for Governor was. I came to see what the office really meant, and how determined my father was in campaigning for it.

As a speaker, he was tremendously dynamic, just as he is today. He really had a way of getting to a crowd and exciting them, because he believed completely in what he was saying. After he had finished speaking, people would just swarm to meet him. It made me very proud.

Mother was turning into quite an effective campaigner herself. Juanita Halstead, her close friend, toured with her and she recalls, "In 1958 she didn't campaign the full campaign. She was a little bit late going out throughout the state with him. But then in 1962, she campaigned from the very beginning. And many times she and I would be in one part of the state, and George and *his* group would be in *another* part of the state.

"She was being entertained and meeting women from all over the state, and I don't think anybody that ever knew her disliked her. She enjoyed meeting people, and her sincerity just reached everybody.

"You know, she liked to fly," Mrs. Halstead reminded me. "She had some lessons before George was elected in '62—maybe four or five hours of instruction—and fully intended going on and getting her license. But things at the Mansion kept her pretty busy, so I think she only took a few lessons afterward.

"But one day, during the 1962 campaign, she and I were flying to a ladies' coffee down at Elba, Alabama. I was piloting the plane. It was March, and it was real windy, even though it was a beautiful day and clear as it could be.

"I was flying a little Tri-Pacer airplane, which is

a very light single-engine plane. And we bumped along, and it was so rough that I was almost sick myself and I was afraid *she* was going to be.

"Suddenly we saw this airport down under us, and I said, 'Lurleen, *I* don't know if this is Elba or *not*. But we're just sure as the dickens gonna *land*. And we'll see what it is.'

"So we landed, and nobody was there to meet us. They had a big hangar there, but there wasn't a sign on the hangar—there was nothing to indicate that it was Elba, Alabama. And she and I even went over to the trash can and tried to find some mail—some letters that would indicate whether we were in Elba or not.

"It took about fifteen or twenty minutes before somebody drove up and acknowledged that we *were* in Elba.

"So Lurleen said, 'Well, there's one thing that's going to happen if George is elected Governor. Elba, Alabama, is going to have a sign on its hangar: ELBA, ALABAMA.' And I haven't been back there, so I don't know if they have their name on their hangar or not."

My father's main opponents in the 1962 primary were former Governor James ("Kissin' Jim") Folsom and a young state senator named Ryan DeGraffenried. "Kissin' Jim" was known to like a drink or two, and my dad made a point of announcing that no liquor would be served in the Mansion if *he* were elected Governor.

Jim Folsom was eliminated in the primary, however. Dad came in first and DeGraffenried was his opponent in the runoff.

On election night our campaign headquarters were in the Jefferson Davis Hotel in Montgomery, as they had been before. But this time everybody was happy and smiling. Dad had polled the biggest vote for Governor that any candidate had ever received, winning 77,000 votes more than his opponent.

When his victory was certain, the whole family was hustled out to a local television station to appear with him while he made a victory statement.

I remember his telling me, "We won, Son!" I was happy and proud of him, as we all were, especially my mother. He went on to trounce his independent opponent in November as expected.

Times were very pleasant for the Wallaces between election and inauguration—particularly for Dad, who was working on his inaugural address. I couldn't recall ever having seen him so content before. He had finally achieved his goal—a goal he'd had since he was fifteen years old.

One of the proudest moments of my boyhood came that fall, after my dad's election as Governor.

I was playing quarterback for the Arrow Rents Pee-wee football team, and I was excited about that because it was the position Dad had played in high school. And Dad came to see me play the last game of the season.

He was standing by the fence, near the end of the game, smoking a cigar. There were several men with him. Our team was behind by 21 to 7. But we had the ball at our 40-yard line. And I ran 60 yards for a touchdown.

I remember running near the sideline and looking over at him, and he was clapping and yelling. That was *his son* running for a touchdown!

My touchdown wasn't enough to win the game, but Dad was very proud of me, and I'll always remember that moment.

We drove home together after the game, both of us in the front seat, and every time he would look over at me and mention my touchdown I'd fairly glow. Because I always tried to get his approval in anything I did, and I was so glad I had made him proud of me. When we got home, Mother was just as excited as he was.

Chapter Seven

I REMEMBER my first visit to the Governor's Mansion after Dad won in 1962. It was before the inauguration, and Mrs. Patterson, Mother's predecessor as First Lady, was helping her get situated.

When I walked in, it just floored me: the ornate Victorian furniture, the huge red-carpeted stairway leading up to the second-floor living quarters, with the grandfather clock where the stairway divided, the twinkling French chandeliers, the two "mirrors of infinity" that reflect each other endlessly in the living room, the formal dining room with its Grecian-themed ceiling, the portraits of the Governors and First Ladies who had lived in the Mansion—and to think that a year earlier we had been living in a crowded low-rent apartment. It was almost too much for an eleven-year-old boy to comprehend.

Two gentlemen from the Mansion staff showed me the house and grounds, and when they took me into the living room one of them said, "Now, if there's a movie that you'd like to see, we'll get it for you."

I said, "Wow! Are you serious?"

They assured me, "Yes, we'll get you the movie."

But I never did ask to have a movie shown at the Mansion. If I wanted to see a picture, I went to see it in a theater, just as I always had.

My father's first inauguration, on January 19, 1963, took place on one of the coldest days of the year. It was a very formal affair, with the men all wearing top hats, striped pants and morning coats, stiff collars and Ascot ties. Even *I* wore a top hat and formal attire. How I hated that stiff collar with its sharp points!

Since it was so cold, Dad and I wore long underwear underneath our rented finery.

As we dressed that morning in the general's house, which we were about to leave for our new home in the Mansion, I remember I was worried whether I would be able to put on all my fancy clothes correctly. But Mother (who had chosen a nice but simple suit for the occasion, as had my sisters) helped both Dad and me to dress.

Eloise, a young black woman who had joined our household to help Mother keep house and help take care of Lee, was as excited as the rest of us. She would be moving into the Mansion with the family, and staying with us until a couple of years ago.

Dad was happy and eager—after all, this was his day. He kept checking up on us as Mother helped us get dressed, and then we all had breakfast and left for the inauguration.

The family was driven to the edge of the downtown section in closed cars, but there we had to exchange the warmth of those cars for the bone-chilling discomfort of open convertibles, as we joined the inaugural parade. We rode very slowly through the downtown streets sitting up on top of the seats, which increased our exposure to the cold winds.

Dad was in the front car with Mother, and we children followed in other cars. I remember I rode with my sister Peggy. I saw a lot of my friends, classmates and teachers in the crowds that lined the parade route, and exchanged excited waves with each acquaintance as I passed.

After driving along Dexter, the main street in Montgomery which leads to the State Capitol, we left our cars where the parking area begins a block from the Capitol and were greeted by Governor Patterson, who escorted Dad the final block to the reviewing stand from which we would watch the rest of the parade. The stand was centered in front of the Capitol.

Of the two men, Dad was by far the more spirited that day. He was striding along jauntily with a big smile on his face, shaking hands with everybody along the way.

On the reviewing stand, there was a podium where Dad stood through most of the parade while the rest of the family sat nearby, mercifully warmed by blankets and electric heaters. Sometimes we would get up and stand with him as he reviewed the bands, marching units and floats. Halfway through the parade, little Lee grew restless and someone took her into the Capitol, where she stayed until we were ready to leave.

We all took special interest in the large float from our own Barbour County, which traced Dad's life from Clio High School football player to attorney, legislator, judge and Governor. I remember it well—and also the band from Clayton. As you can imagine, it wasn't a very large band, because Clayton itself isn't very large. But we did have a band, and my father was very proud to see it there. These were our hometown people.

There was a sign reading "In God We Trust" on the reviewing stand, directly in front of where we stood. And my father took the oath of office on the exact spot where Jefferson Davis stood when he was inaugurated as President of the Confederacy. My mother stood behind him, and I stood behind her with Bobbi and Peggy. Wherever we looked from the reviewing stand, there were people as far as we could see.

Although I was trembling from the cold, I felt tremendously proud of my father as he repeated the oath of office. His face was very serious as he took the oath, and I just knew that he believed every word he was saying.

After that he delivered his inaugural address, which was nationally reported and whose climax and summary is still quoted by friend and foe alike:

"I draw the line in the dust and toss the gauntlet before the feet of tyranny. And I say, 'Segregation now! Segregation tomorrow! Segregation forever!' "

Who could have dreamed on that frigid day in 1963, as the huge crowd cheered and applauded my father's words, that a decade later George Wallace would still be Governor, and that he would have presided during his terms of office over the end of segregation as a way of life in Alabama? Certainly not my father himself! But we live, we grow, we accept—and we change. The past is gone, and without regrets for its passing.

When my father's inaugural address was over, we went into the Capitol and entered Room 100, the Governor's office, where we had pictures made and there was a reception for the immediate family, the cabinet and friends. Dad was going around the room talking to everybody, and still in the best of spirits.

While he was busy greeting people, my mother and sisters and I, who were very hungry by that time, went across the hall to Room 101, where a buffet had been laid out, and we gratefully filled up on sandwiches. My father remained in the Governor's office, and I don't recall that he ever ate again during that long day and night.

There was an inaugural ball that evening in Montgomery's Garrett Coliseum. We drove there with a police escort, in a long black 1959 limousine Governor Patterson had used. But Dad hardly ever used the limousine again, preferring a simple black Ford.

The first dance at the ball was Dad's favorite song— you guessed it—*Stars Fell on Alabama*. They had a lead-out for this dance. The Governor and First Lady led a procession to the center of the dance floor, then turned in one direction, while the next couple turned in the opposite direction, and so on until a circle had been formed, after which the dancing began. Following my parents onto the floor were members of the family and then cabinet members and others.

I danced with my sister Peggy—we always seemed to be paired off—and I remember she kept trying to lead. I didn't like that, so I tried to lead *her*. Then she tugged at me, and I tugged at her, and we exchanged a few sharp words—with smiles on our faces so that nobody would see the Governor's children were having a disagreement. Not only were there other dancers around us, but the stands were open to the public. We remember that episode now and laugh about it, because we really didn't mind dancing with each other despite our tug-of-war.

My father and mother danced for a while, and then sat in the bunting-draped Governor's box, from which they viewed the other dancers and received the congratulations of friends who came over in a steady procession to chat. The ball went on until after midnight, by which time the new Governor and his family were thoroughly exhausted.

When I woke up in the Governor's Mansion, it took me a moment to realize that I wasn't still in the general's house. But when I saw where I was, it was a nice feeling. I liked living in the Mansion from the very first. I had my own room, first on the right from the stairway—a high-ceilinged room like all the others, with two single beds and a desk that was built into the wall, shelves for books, a large closet and my own bathroom, which was quite a luxury for me. I promptly moved my Little Golden Book Encyclopedia onto the shelves, along with my schoolbooks, and had soon added such other personal touches to the room as a record player, a television set, and some model planes and cars that I had put together.

Peggy's room was next to mine. Then there was a large open space with a television set and a sofa, which I guess you could call our private family living room, since the Mansion was open to tourists downstairs seven days a week by my father's decision. Then came Dad's and Mother's room—no separate bedrooms for them. After that was Bobbi Jo's room, which she occupied until her marriage in 1964, and then Lee's room.

The rooms have been considerably rearranged since that time, and the second floor has been remodeled since my father was injured, so that he has a private office there now next to his and Cornelia's bedroom. My own room is now on the other side of the house from where it was, overlooking the patio in the rear.

Then as now, the family ate in a small private dining room downstairs, hidden away directly behind the grand stairway. Only rarely did we eat in the large formal dining room, which was designed for more official functions.

The food at the Mansion has always been good.

Mother and Dad liked country-style cooking, and that's what we still have. We eat a lot of fried chicken, as well as roast beef, steak and pork chops, with such vegetables as black-eyed peas, corn, butter beans, okra, and home-grown tomatoes people have sent us.

When we first moved into the Mansion, we had liver once a week, and that's the only thing I wouldn't eat. I much preferred the fried chicken to anything else. My mother supervised the menus, as I think all the First Ladies have done. Cornelia does so today.

At the table in the private dining room I discovered that each place had a buzzer you could touch with your foot if you wanted something (Dad's has now been moved up so that it is operable by hand.) Most of the help at the Mansion are trusties of both races from the state prison, and they have always served us with gentleness, dependability and good humor. It's considered a choice assignment among the prisoners, and they really seem to enjoy working there. A very informal, easygoing atmosphere reigns in the kitchen, where the help often chat with a member of the family who may drop in for a cup of coffee. State troopers maintain the Mansion's security and help look after the family's needs.

One of the reasons I liked living in the Mansion was the presence of those state troopers, who became my friends. They and the others on the Mansion staff were there to accommodate the family, and when we moved in that was new and exciting to me. Whatever I wanted, they would try to help me, and they would kid with me and play with me. I really enjoyed it.

From the beginning, I would have friends stay over-night in my room. The Mansion has a large circular drive-way with a grassy yard in the center, and we used to play football out there. We really kicked the lawn up quite a bit, just as I had done with my friends in Clayton years earlier.

My friends used to marvel at the Mansion when they'd come over. And I did myself at first—it was very exciting. But after a while I became used to it, because it was my home. And I wanted my friends to get used to it, too.

However, when I'd bring someone over, he would just stand around and stare, awestruck. And I'd have to say, "Come on! Let's go! Let's go!"

If I'd say, "Let's go downstairs," my friend would be afraid to touch anything in the public rooms. And if we were going through a door, he'd ask, "Where does *this* go?"

I didn't want my friends to feel that way, but it went on for some time, much to my dismay.

Col. E. C. Dothard, now the Alabama Director of Public Safety, had known and admired Dad since 1957, when they met in Barbour County, where the Colonel was a new state trooper: "I'd never met a judge before, but he made me feel like I'd been away and come home!" He was still a trooper when he was assigned to protect our family shortly after the inauguration.

He explains: "The Governor's Mansion was fired on in April, 1963. Somebody drove by and fired a pistol shot at the Mansion, and I was called in the next day and went to work for the Governor's security." He helped protect the family until my mother died in 1968, and served Dad again after 1970.

It was Colonel Dothard who bought me my first guitar early in 1963. Dad had him go with me to the Sears store, and I picked out a twenty-nine-dollar Silvertone acoustic guitar.

When Dad saw the guitar, which had been bought

at my urgent request, he picked it up and showed me three or four chords on it. And he played them very well. I thought that was terrific, not realizing they were just about the only chords he knew. At the time, his ability to play the guitar at all amazed me more than his political achievements, because it was something I could relate to more closely. For I was really starting to get interested in music and was anxious to learn more about it. You might say Dad was my first teacher, but he couldn't take me very far.

There was a black man named Jim, one of the trusties at the Mansion, who played guitar and influenced me with my music because he knew a lot of chords. And another black trusty named Robert, whom either my dad or Uncle Jack had sent to prison, played the blues. When I got my guitar, Robert helped me with it. I've seen him since; he works for Bobbi Jo's husband now that he's finished serving his sentence.

I used to hear Robert playing in his room—he'd have his window open, with just a screen on it—and he'd be playing nice chords that I wished I could play.

He didn't have his own guitar at first; he was using Jim's. Then he played mine some, and soon he bought one at a pawn shop. (Of course, trusties didn't earn a lot of money.) After that, Robert and I played guitar together. I was just learning, but my ambition was always to be better than he was on the guitar.

When I saw Robert again recently, I played for him, and I can do some things on the guitar that *he* can't. He was self-taught and stayed right where he was, while I kept learning. But he still sounds mighty good.

When I could play my Silvertone fairly well, I used to play for my mother. She would come into my room when she heard my guitar, and I would do some old Hank Williams songs for her. I remember I played *Your Cheatin' Heart,* and we sang that together.

I also had a record of Floyd Tilman's called *Slippin' Around* that was one of Dad's favorite songs. When I was playing that on my record player, Daddy used to come into my room and listen to it. And Dad and Mother danced in my room one night to that song. It was a beautiful moment that I'll never forget.

Although living in the Mansion was exciting at first, after a few years I realized that it also had its disadvantages along with its many pleasures.

I came to see that it was like living in a fishbowl. Since the upstairs is the only living quarters, you can't come down the front stairs unless you have time to visit with the tourists, who have every right to be there because the Mansion belongs to the people of the state.

I'm used to it now, and if I want to use the grand staircase instead of the private stairway in the back of the house, I just walk down, shake hands with the people and go on my way.

But one morning when I was twelve, I forgot that the front stairs were in public view. I came down the grand staircase in my pajamas, not even thinking, on my way to eat breakfast. And I had a grand shock, because there was a troop of Girl Scouts at the foot of the stairs looking up at me. That's really embarrassing when you're twelve years old!

So I quickly turned around and hurried back up the stairs, while the Girl Scouts all giggled.

But my mother tried to make our lives as normal as possible despite the fact that we were involved in the political game and living in a public place. She tried to spend as much time with us as she could, even though she had her own duties as First Lady. Dad was out speaking a lot as Governor, particularly as the years passed, and she tried to make up to us for his absences.

Everyone around the Mansion just loved her. She spoke to everybody, and from the start she was interested in what anybody around there had to say, whether it was a trusty or the trooper at the gate. When she was alive, there was just a magic feeling throughout the Mansion. You could sense it.

She really tried to make the Mansion a home for us. There was nothing she could do or *wanted* to do about the daily flow of tourists, but she tried to keep our own *private* lives as close as she could. Birthdays, Christmas, events like that stayed very important. So did going to church. She *loved* going to church.

I remember my mother and father were at St. James Methodist Church one Sunday morning while they were living in the Mansion, and he wasn't wearing a hearing aid yet. He was leaning forward, listening to the preacher, and he had his hand cupped to his left ear. He wears glasses sometimes for reading, and he had them on that day.

As he strained forward to hear, his glasses slipped down on the edge of his nose, and he looked so funny that my mother started laughing in church.

Dad looked over to see what Mother was laughing at, and when he realized what it was, he saw that it was making her laugh so hard she was trying to restrain herself to keep from being disrespectful of her surroundings.

When he saw how much it amused her, he strained forward even more, and the glasses slipped precariously close to falling off. He, too, meant no disrespect—but I think he's kind of a ham sometimes.

Even though she and Dad were often on public display, my mother didn't receive any bad publicity. She handled herself very well with the press and public. She knew what to say, and what not to say.

And she never talked to us about not doing anything that might bring discredit on our father or the family. She never had to, because she had reared us well.

Even though Dad had quite a few speaking engagements as Governor, the family saw more of him than when he had been a candidate. He went to his office in the Capitol every day and was usually home at night. The whole family got together at dinner. And Dad seemed very happy that we were all enjoying a fairly normal life once again.

Mother adapted very well from the country life in Clayton to being First Lady. She was a very *gracious* First Lady. Several articles were written about how well she handled the various official functions at the Mansion— receptions and ladies' teas and banquets. She wasn't a showy person. She was very genuine and down-to-earth, and everyone liked that. Although she and Dad didn't drink and there was no liquor in the Mansion, soft drinks and tea and coffee seemed to serve very well in its place when guests were entertained.

So our life in the Mansion was pleasant and as normal as possible—even though we had to get used to having our pictures snapped by tourists every time we stepped outside.

Speaking of pictures, a couple of years ago I was living in my own apartment for a while, and one night

I'd been up late practicing with my musical group. I decided to spend the night at the Mansion but found that some visitor was using my old room.

So I went downstairs and went to sleep on the sofa in the sun room, which is the only public room that has contemporary furniture. I had told the trooper to wake me up at 7 A.M., and he did. I said, "Okay, I'll get up." But I went back to sleep.

Eventually I heard a noise and woke up. And there was a group of ladies standing around me and taking my picture! This time I was fully clothed, thank goodness.

Although I was very young during my first years in the Mansion, I did hear about my father's achievements as Governor. I knew he was bringing new industry to our state and was responsible for a vastly expanded interstate highway system. He built fifteen new trade schools and fourteen junior colleges, and provided free textbooks for all school children. There were many other achievements as well.

Despite the fact that his views on segregation and states' rights would bring him into conflict with the President and the federal government during his very first year in office, my father was on good personal terms with President John F. Kennedy. He has a picture that was taken of the two of them during President Kennedy's trip to Alabama in 1963 to visit the Huntsville Space Center.

Their meeting was warm and pleasant—even jocular. When they went to sit in the helicopter, Dad said, "Mr. President, you may sit on the left, and I'll sit on the right."

During the summer of 1963 we bought a nice cottage at Lake Martin, thirty miles north of Montgomery, and fixed it up so that it was very comfortable. We had a houseboat and a motorboat for water skiing. Mother liked the lake very much and spent a lot of time there with my sisters and me.

My father would come up occasionally, but it was hard to get him to rest during this period and the years immediately following. He was very active, getting his various programs through and giving speeches, first in Alabama and then around the nation as his fame grew. By then I understood that you can't *make* a man rest. He's got to do what he *has* to do.

My mother, of course, indulged her passion for fishing at the lake, fishing from the bank by herself as early as 2 A.M. with the aid of a light. The rest of us would rise at a later hour to swim and ski and fish and thoroughly enjoy ourselves.

Eloise was there to cook and to help Mother take care of Lee. So Mother was really able to rest up from her duties as First Lady. She'd visit the lake as much as she could, staying a week or more at a time in the summer and for occasional weekends during the school year.

By the summer of 1963 I already knew that my father was a pretty controversial Governor—that his inaugural address defending segregation had drawn national attention. That summer he became even *more* controversial, as the family discovered one day at Lake Martin while we watched him on television.

He went to the University of Alabama at Tuscaloosa one morning in June and stood dramatically in front of a doorway to protest the admission of the first two black students to the university.

The national government had decided the students should be admitted, and had a federal judge's court order to that effect.

My mother, my sisters and I clustered around the television set at our cottage, and Mother watched nervously as Assistant Attorney General Nicholas Katzenbach approached Dad, who was standing at a lectern and threw up his hand to stop him.

After an exchange of words between my father and Katzenbach, the Assistant Attorney General left and my father disappeared into the building. When the commanding general of the Alabama National Guard returned four hours later, Dad returned and accepted his salute. Dad was informed that the guard had been federalized. Then he read a statement and stepped aside, formally yielding to federal power, and the students were enrolled.

My mother relaxed as the tense confrontation came to a peaceful conclusion. But my father's action brought him a flood of mail from people who understood what he'd been trying to do—and a flock of speaking invitations from colleges all over the United States who wanted to hear him explain his views. He accepted many of them, from such campuses as Oregon, UCLA and Harvard, often being greeted by hostile demonstrators.

Actually he had wanted to show by his "schoolhouse door" stand how far the federal government would go to take over an institution in a conflict with the state government—and, as usual, my father had favored local control, using a unique and memorable way of getting his point across.

The confrontation at the University of Alabama has really been a black mark against my father in many people's eyes. It has taken a long time for people to realize that his main interest in the matter was local control—a control which at that time meant segregation of the races to him, although it no longer does. You know, he has all but given his life to changing the direction of this country, trying to cut down on the power of the federal government.

In this he considers himself the spokesman for the common people, and I believe he's really one of the few politicians today who has the average workingman's interests at heart. He has never been popular with the power elite.

Although President Kennedy and his brother, Attorney General Robert Kennedy, had come into direct conflict with my father when he resisted the enrollment of black students at the university, it was a governmental confrontation with no personal hostility involved. And Dad was very upset that November when President Kennedy was assassinated.

I was terribly shocked, too, when I heard the news of the shooting. I was in my sixth-grade class at Bellingrath when our principal announced the news over the intercom. I remember the girl behind me started crying, and I tried to comfort her, even though I myself was stunned.

I didn't find out until I got home that the President had died. I heard the news on television. And from that point on I realized that the same fate might befall my own father.

I think Mother began to be worried, too, but she didn't show it. She accompanied my father to President Kennedy's funeral.

Despite the assassination, the protection given my father was not increased. It was felt that he was already well guarded by the Alabama state troopers. But my own fears for my father's safety continued, and they increased in 1968 with the assassinations of Martin Luther King, Jr., and Robert Kennedy. By then I realized that the same thing could very *easily* happen to Dad.

I really admired Bobby Kennedy, as I did President Kennedy. Jack Paar was very close to the Kennedys, I know, and he had some films on television about Bobby's family life—how outgoing he and his family were, and how much they loved athletics, which has always been one of my interests. So I felt especially close to them, and his death hit me hard.

At school I was treated no differently than other boys during the first few years my father was Governor. I got along well with my classmates and teachers and conformed to every rule. In the sixth grade my only distinction was that I was captain of the patrol boys, with lieutenants, sergeants, corporals and privates serving under me as crossing guards. I proudly wore my gray patrol uniform to classes every day.

I was also in a city marching team called the Rebel Lancers, which had two boys from each school in it. We had a Marine sergeant who drilled us in formations every Thursday. We went to Washington in 1963 to march in a parade, and we appeared all over Montgomery.

My sixth-grade teacher, Mrs. McQueen, was very musical and really helped and inspired me. We used to sing in her class, and I had a ukulele group that played for several events, strumming such songs as *Five Foot Two, Eyes of Blue*.

My father first ran for President of the United States in 1964, when he entered spring primaries in Wisconsin, Indiana and Maryland. And he did very well in them, which surprised a lot of people.

In Wisconsin he won almost 35 percent of the Democratic vote. In Indiana he won almost 30 percent. And he nearly won the primary in Maryland, with some 45 percent of the ballots.

Clearly the voters were beginning to realize what George Wallace was all about, even if they had never been in Alabama. And they were casting their votes for him in significant numbers.

He campaigned for local control of democratic institutions, and against encroachment by the federal government on the lives of private citizens. To him it was a constitutional matter, and not a question of repressing blacks. I'm sure he never considered himself a racist, nor did we in the family think of him that way.

I was very proud that he was doing so well nationally, as any son would be, although I realized some people thought it strange to have a southern Governor running in northern primaries. But the people of Alabama liked the idea of having a native son representing their views in other states.

Dad wasn't gone from home for long periods of time during the 1964 primaries. He would leave, make some speeches, and return. I didn't accompany him, because I was in school. But sometimes Mother went with him.

She saw how controversial he was—and how easily controversy could flare into violence—when he spoke at a college campus during the 1964 primary campaign. She was in the back seat of a car with him and the car was nearly turned over by about fifty students. They rocked it back and forth and broke some of the windows. The security men told me later that she always kept a smile on her face but was really very nervous, and that Daddy was very cool, as he always is when that sort of thing happens. He showed no outward emotion at all.

When they got back to Montgomery, Mother admitted to Bobbi and Peggy and me that the car-rocking incident had upset her. I was glad she and Dad were all right, but I, too, realized that from that point on anything could happen because Dad had become so controversial.

He was glad to speak at northern colleges when they would let him speak. And I've heard him say that a certain element is always talking about freedom of speech, but when *he* wants to speak they won't let him talk. I think that's pretty hypocritical of them. Whether you agree or not, you can sit still and listen, and maybe you'll learn something you didn't know before. And maybe my dad will learn something in the question-and-answer period. He's a strong believer in trying to work things out, and I don't think there's ever been a time he thought he was always right about everything. He always wants to hear the other side. He's said that publicly, and I've heard him say it in private.

Dad didn't go to the Democratic National Convention that summer—it was the Johnson and Goldwater year. But he continued to speak all over the nation, and it was harder than ever that year to get him to visit the lake with us and relax. We were all resigned to that by now.

Not only did Dad travel around the nation. The nation's press was increasingly converging on Alabama to do stories about George Wallace and even about his family.

We became increasingly aware that Dad was a newsmaker when television crews and writers from the large national magazines began appearing at the Mansion.

I met some of the press people from the large magazines. Some of them would come and eat with us at the Mansion. I began to have a small distaste for certain writers, because they would be so nice there and then they would write a story that was very slanted—things like what a sloppy eater my dad supposedly was and similar ridiculous statements. They would take his remarks out of context and generally turn his language around. I think some writers tried to make him come across as pretty ignorant. So I began to distrust writers in general.

Even local papers in Montgomery were against my father at that point and they still are, though it's not unanimous. I wasn't reading editorials at that age, but when I was two or three years older I began to read them and see what they were saying about him.

It used to bother me at first when they were against him. I asked him, "Why don't you answer them? Why would they want to do this?"

But he told me calmly, "Son, don't worry about it. That's part of the game."

After that I'd still read the editorials but they wouldn't bother me.

Often I'd see Dad pick up a paper and read it and then put it down, and it seemed not to annoy him at all if he'd been criticized. I don't think bad press has *ever* bothered him, really. I think it bothered Mother, though, when the press attacked him. But as usual she would try not to let us know it.

In the seventh grade I played football and basketball on junior high teams after school, but by then my parents were so busy that I can't remember them coming to one game during that 1964–65 school year. And Dad was so involved in politics that I don't recall our sitting down together and discussing sports as we had done in the past.

But he approved when I ventured into school politics

myself in the seventh grade and was elected vice-president of the student council. And both my parents were pleased that I always had good grades. I spent a lot of time with my good friend, Ronnie Wise, and got to know his family well. His house was like a second home to me, and I often had dinner there.

That year I had an older friend named Chris Creesman, who was in the Air Force. He was a drummer, and since I played guitar, we appeared together in the school auditorium for assemblies. I remember playing *Wipeout,* for instance. Those were my first public appearances as a guitarist, but I wasn't nervous even then. I enjoyed it.

My mother really encouraged my music, and sometimes she'd sing while I played at home—mostly Hank Williams things. We got together on *Your Cheatin' Heart, Jambalaya* and *I'm So Lonesome I Could Cry.* She had a very nice soprano voice.

When Dad wasn't away speaking, he'd come home at night and we'd all eat together. Then I'd go to my room to study, and often he'd come in and ask how my schoolwork was coming along.

Sometimes he'd sit in the upstairs living room and watch TV. He always was interested in the news. And he liked Lawrence Welk. Personally, of course, I was more into the Beatles. But I think he liked Welk because some of his music had been popular when Dad was in the service. So Dad enjoyed the show and the songs.

Mom liked Lawrence Welk, too, and she enjoyed The Dean Martin Show. She really liked Dean Martin's singing.

It was in 1964 that my sister, Bobbi Jo, married Jim Parsons, who owns a construction company in Birmingham. Their wedding was held at St. James Methodist Church, with a reception following in the Mansion. Bobbi's wedding was the first break in our family circle, but we all approved of her choice of Jim as her husband, even though it meant we wouldn't be seeing her nearly so much anymore.

Bobbi Jo's wedding had made Mother something of an expert in such matters—and in 1965 she willingly used that expertise in the service of a friend.

"One of my daughters was getting married," Juanita Halstead recalls, "and Lurleen was down here one morning and she said, 'You know, you just look awfully tired. You're trying to *do* too much. Let *me* take charge of this wedding and this reception.'

"And I said, 'Well, *you* have too much to do, too.' But she insisted, 'No, I don't *have* as much to do as you do.' "

At that time, of course, my mother was busy with all her duties as First Lady. But she insisted on helping a friend just the same.

"And she did!" Juanita recalls. "She really just took over and did the planning of the wedding and reception and handled all the responsibilities. It was this unselfishness that I think endeared her to everybody who knew her."

For those who loved my mother, however, 1965 was nevertheless a tragic milestone. For it marked the beginning of her heartbreaking fight against cancer, although for a time it seemed that she had won the battle.

Late in 1965 she told us children that she had a malignancy—that was what she called it. She had gone to St. Margaret's Hospital in Montgomery for a checkup, and it had been discovered that she had abdominal cancer. But she didn't let us see that she was alarmed about it.

I knew almost nothing about cancer at that point. I just knew it was something bad. Of course, I learned a lot about it from then on.

In January, 1966, she entered St. Margaret's for cancer surgery. The doctors performed a hysterectomy and then gave her a clean bill of health. They thought they had caught the cancer in time. My mother took them at their word, and so did the rest of the family. There really was nothing else we could do but believe them and hope that nothing changed in the future.

Had she known the tragedy that lay ahead, Mother would never have taken the remarkable step of running for Governor of Alabama.

Chapter Eight

MY MOTHER was not the kind of woman you would have expected to be a Governor. But she learned fast—because she had to.

By nature she was shy and retiring. Juanita Halstead recounts a prophetic incident from my father's 1962 campaign that reflects both her shyness and how she overcame it to win the people's approval and their love.

"When George was running for Governor in 1962, Lurleen and I were down in Mobile," Juanita remembers, "and one of his opponents, MacDonald Gallion, had withdrawn from the race. The people who had been supporting Gallion wanted to speak to George and offer their support to him.

"But George was in north Alabama and just couldn't get away, because he had some commitments up there that made it impossible for him to go.

"He wanted Lurleen to appear in his place, but she was hoping that someone else would come down. Because this was when she was really not too politically inclined herself. But when George asked her if she would go, she of course said yes.

"Nevertheless, as we walked along the street in Mobile, she said she'd get scared appearing before those people and she was sure her knees would knock.

"She laughed and said, 'My knees are knocking *now!* Do you hear 'em? What am I going to *say?*'

"But she had that beautiful smile on her face. And one of the fellows with us said, 'You don't have to say a word. All you have to do is stand up there and smile. Man, you'll win every vote!' "

But of course it wasn't only her smile that made my mother an effective campaigner and a good Governor. She quickly learned the issues and campaigned on them, and once she was Governor she mastered her job thoroughly and became an effective chief executive. But her charm and humility did help her immensely in winning people over.

In the fall of 1965 my father tried to persuade the Alabama State Legislature to pass and submit to the voters a constitutional amendment which would change the state's succession law so that he could run for a second term. "The issue is the right of the Alabama people to vote to amend or not to amend their own constitution," he insisted, and urged, "Let the *people* speak!"

But the legislature refused to pass such an amendment, even after he had called it into special session for that purpose. This meant he could only serve one term and must then be replaced by another Governor.

Dad felt he was a good Governor, and he frankly *enjoyed* being Governor, a position for which he had prepared himself since the age of fifteen. He found great satisfaction in the work, and felt he had done a great deal for the state and could do more in the future, if permitted.

He did not want to wait four years, as prescribed by the state constitution, before running again, as that would completely destroy the momentum of progress he had established in Alabama. It would also hamper him in his continuing efforts to extend his voice and influence to the national scene.

At first the situation seemed hopeless, and I could see that he was very unhappy and frustrated. There appeared to be no answer to the problem.

And then it occurred to him that Mother, who shared his philosophies completely, might run in his place, campaigning on the promise that he would be her principal adviser and would thus be able to continue his policies through her.

Mother was skeptical when Dad first suggested that she run for Governor. But she thought it over for a few months. Meanwhile, she underwent her first cancer surgery, believed it to be a success, and grew more optimistic about life and the idea that she might indeed run successfully for public office.

One day my mother told my sisters and me that she and Dad had discussed the possibility of her running for Governor—and that she had decided to run.

I thought if that was what she wanted to do, it was fine with me. I didn't realize at the time that it would mean I'd be seeing much less of her because of her added responsibilities as campaigner and Governor—but that came about.

Contrary to what some people said at the time, it was my mother's decision to run. She was not pushed into it. My father thought of the idea first, it's true. But once she had decided to make the race, nothing could sway her—not even Dad himself.

For at one point he changed his mind and decided she should not make the race. "No, Lurleen, I don't want you to run," he told her, thinking that would be that.

He was worried about the effect the pressures of an election campaign would have on her, especially coming so soon after her operation. He thought the traveling and the speeches, which he was so used to, would be too much for her if they campaigned together all over the state as planned.

But she replied, "I want to run! And I'll be disappointed if I can't." She refused to change her mind, much to my father's surprise.

Comedian Dave Gardner, a longtime family friend, and his wife, Miss Millie, tell an amusing story about this particular time in my parents' lives.

"Lurleen hadn't officially announced," Dave remembers, "but it was in the works. Miss Millie and I were having lunch with the Governor in the basement commissary at the State Capitol.

"Now, if he meets you five times a day, he's gonna shake hands with you each time. I think he *still* probably shakes hands with *you*, George."

I agreed, "He always shakes hands with me whenever he sees me."

"So he's going down the food line at the cafeteria, shaking hands with his own help, Man!" Dave continued. "Miss Millie and I had already gone through the line, and the security man had brought his food to the table for him. There were ham and raisins and the tomato ketchup bottle. You know, that's the way to find him—just follow the tomato ketchup bottle."

Miss Millie added, "We were waiting for him to sit down to eat, and I finally went over and got him."

"So he was sitting there eating," Dave went on, "and I said, 'Well, now, what are you gonna do, George, when Lurleen gets elected and she takes over *on the square?*'

"It had never entered his mind that she might decide to run the state without him. And he said, 'Huh?' and dropped a whole forkful of ham and raisins."

Miss Millie laughed, "All he had left on his fork was one raisin!"

Soon after that—on February 24, 1966—my mother officially announced her candidacy to succeed my father as Governor of Alabama. Although I sang and played the guitar at her kickoff rally at the city auditorium in Montgomery, I didn't play any more during that campaign because I was busy with school.

Mother and Dad traveled the state, making speeches everywhere. In the beginning, she would speak for a few minutes and then my dad would speak for about forty-five minutes. But that changed as the campaign progressed.

She would introduce him by saying, "If you elect me, he will be my number one adviser." And she promised to pay him a dollar a year. It was understood that he would make the major decisions, although in consultation with her, and in that way my father would continue to be the decisive influence in state affairs. Dad also made it clear he might well be campaigning for President again in 1968.

As they prepared to speak at the first town on the road, Dad was very concerned about the crowd, wondering whether it would be large or not. For he was used to drawing huge crowds, but he really didn't know how this new arrangement would work. The nation had only had two female Governors in the past, one of them appointed, and my mother would be the first for Alabama if she were elected. There was really no way of knowing how the voters would take to the idea, and some people were already making jokes about it.

Much to Dad's relief, the crowd was very large, and as a candidate Mother outdrew him in bringing out the people all over the state. Of course, now they were getting two Wallaces instead of one, and they seemed to like the idea.

We children didn't travel with our parents much during that campaign. If there was a statewide television hookup in, say, Birmingham or Mobile, then we would be there and sit on the stage. But in a Governor's race you're hitting five or six cities a day, and that was impossible for us to do and keep up with our studies.

Mother found the campaign exhausting, and she would come back to the Mansion very tired.

She was very self-conscious about making her speeches, because she had never been to college, although she graduated from high school at fifteen and went to business school.

She would rehearse her speeches carefully, saying them to me or to some of her close friends. But I think as the campaign progressed she became an *excellent* speaker, because what she said was very sincere—very genuine.

Dad, who usually writes his own speeches, helped write hers at first, but she got to where she could write one herself, and sometimes combined parts of various speeches, although it was all very new to her. Usually, of course, they repeated their speeches around the state, except for television appearances.

Although Mother was very unsure of herself at first,

she grew more confident when she saw how well people accepted her. They admired my father, they were for him, and they *wanted* Mother to succeed.

She came to enjoy campaigning, because she loved people, and that's the key to being a public servant: you have to like people. I have some pictures of her shaking hands in Montgomery after a speech, and from her expression you could tell how happy she was to see everyone. And she was never too busy to shake hands with *anybody,* or stand and talk with individual voters.

C. J. Hartley of Tuscaloosa, my mother's hometown, has worked in Dad's campaigns and was with Mother's campaign in 1966. And he told me recently, "Tuscaloosa County has always voted against Governor George, and it voted *for* Governor Lurleen. I know when the '66 campaign started, Governor George would always make the speeches. But by the time we got halfway into the campaign, Governor Lurleen was making the speeches and was doing one helluva good job." It's true that Mother did campaign alone for several days when Dad was grounded by a virus—and this gave her much greater confidence. After Dad's return, her speeches preceding his became much longer than they had been before, with more ad libs.

"She had no problem whatsoever in communicating with the people," C. J. continued. "It wasn't a highfalutin' political talk with a bunch of promises. She talked to the people and they believed every word she said.

"At any rate, before the end of that campaign there was no question in anyone's mind but that she was going to be Governor and that she was going to be a good Governor," C. J. Hartley concluded.

Even with her heavy campaign schedule, Mother

tried to get home and spend as much time as she could with us. But we were having to learn to get along on our own most of the time.

By now we were pretty well used to sharing our parents, and even ourselves, with the public. "And yet," my sister Peggy mused recently, "we *have* been a closely-knit family, in a strange sort of way. It's not like a family that has three meals together every day and worships on Sunday. It's been such a *hectic* life!

"You know, when Mother was alive, we used to have to make a mental list of what we wanted to ask her when she was home, because she was gone so much.

"And living in the public eye is just a real difficult thing to do, as far as the personal family life goes. I think for me, and I'm sure for you, too, George, the older you get, the more you realize that it's *not* going to change, no matter *how* bad you want to have three meals together— no matter *how* bad you want to worship on Sunday together—it just can't *be*.

"For me it has a lot of disadvantages *and* advantages, but I think that for *your* children, George, you want a *more* closely-knit family, as I do. We've been close—but, as I said, it's been in such an *odd* way! And you really can't make up for the frequent separations. You just have to swing with the punches, you just really do."

How do you do that? For one thing, you try to keep busy on your own. Luckily for me, I was occupied with my music during my mother's campaign, and gave up football and basketball that year to concentrate on practicing my guitar, much to my coaches' surprise.

Col. E. C. Dothard was in charge of our family's security for so long that he saw my sisters and me grow up. And he told me, "What stands out in *my* mind is the fact that, except for Bobbi Jo, you were reared in an atmosphere of being *watched*. Anything that you did or said was written about. If one of you got a dog or something happened in school, it was always in the papers. But I'd say you remained unspoiled through it all; you'd always mind me as quick as you would your own folks.

"But I think that being watched all the time probably bothered *you,* George, more than it did the rest," Colonel Dothard said frankly. "You were rough 'n' tough, and you liked to be just like one of the other boys."

And then he recalled, "Even in school, when we'd get threats on the children in the family, we'd assign troopers to actually be outside your classrooms. This would last usually a few weeks. And usually what would bring it to a halt, you remember, was the fact that you children protested to your folks, and we felt that the danger was past and we'd pull 'em off.

"Take Peggy Sue, especially," he added. "Sometimes when she was dating we had to have somebody follow her."

"I bet it made the *boy* feel strange," I mused.

"Yeah!" he laughed.

And then the conversation turned to my parents as campaigners . . . and as people.

"Governor Wallace is the most unusual person I've ever known," Colonel Dothard said. "He can remember *everybody.* He remembers people he met in 1958! Remembers their name, remembers who was with them, and remembers what they talked about . . . and what they had to eat.

"Anybody he meets, he remembers, which is a *real* asset in a campaign, to call everybody by *name.* If they've been sick, he remembers that. If their *children* are sick, he remembers *that.*

"His image has been bad in other areas of the country, but I have never, in the years that I've known him, heard him say anything to any person, including the black convicts who work at the Mansion, to embarrass them in any way or even get on them in any way. That's unpleasant to him. If it came down to one of the convicts getting out of line or having to be replaced, Governor *Lurleen* handled *that*. That was something he wouldn't do."

I noted, "A lot of people don't realize how compassionate he is."

"And thoughtful," Colonel Dothard added. "It's unusual, with the position he's been in all these years, to *be* so thoughtful and compassionate.

"I think the reason he's popular is that people sense that he's sincere. When he tells a person he's glad to see them, he really *is* glad to see them. When he puts that smile on and shakes their hand, they know he *means* it. It's not just a politician talking. He's sincere and he always has been.

"And of course your mother, she was one of the finest people that I've ever met. She was a real easygoing person, easy to work for. Had a good sense of humor! We enjoyed being with her, and we enjoyed campaigning with her.

"She could always find something to laugh at! Governor George is very serious, and when we campaigned, the campaign was *it*. But she was different. She saw the humor in different things.

"Of course, campaigning in this state is hard, especially if you campaign with George Wallace, because he believes in six speeches a day. He's been campaigning enough to know that's necessary, and he has a system about it. In other words, you'll drive from county to county and courthouse to courthouse.

"But it was quite a bit of stress on *her* to get up and make five speeches a day with a rally at night. And that was all through the sixty-seven counties.

"It was tiring to *me*," Colonel Dothard admitted. "Back then I was about thirty-five years old, and I was exhausted—and I didn't make a speech! But her sense of humor kept her going. She'd laugh and never complain.

"I could see that she was exhausted, though. I would go in the motel at night and she could barely walk up the stairs, she was so tired."

I'll never forget the night my mother won the primary election. Her campaign headquarters were at the Jefferson Davis Hotel, as my father's had been, and that was where we heard the returns. Mother received 480,841 votes—54 percent of the total—easily outdistancing nine male opponents and avoiding a runoff. In the 1962 Democratic primary, Dad's vote total had been 207,062, for 33 percent of the vote. So she had more than doubled his mark.

Dad gave her a victory kiss and we all surrounded her proudly. She went to television station WSFA, where she was interviewed and thanked people for their support. She was pretty emotional that night because of the huge vote of confidence she had received. She had grown up on a farm and never dreamed of being Governor, and there she was, winning the primary, which meant that winning the November election should be easy. And yet she campaigned vigorously in the general election campaign as well, taking no chances against an unusually formidable Republican opponent and a strong independent contender.

That fall, which was my ninth-grade year, I had joined a musical group as their lead singer, and we called ourselves George Wallace, Jr., and the Governor's Four. I was only fourteen, but the others in the group were all Air Force men, stationed at nearby bases. They'd been playing for years and they were excellent. We really didn't need the family name to get work, but at that age I frankly didn't know any better, so we picked what seemed like a clever name.

We traveled around the state in a station wagon on weekends, playing at dances, and word of the Air Force men's musical ability soon spread so that we were packing them in. I managed to keep up the vocal end of the group, and we worked out a whole show, complete with routines. We made really good money by taking a percentage of the gate. I had met them through Bob Harmon, who was then my manager. He had a morning musical show on Montgomery television and had heard them on a telethon. We practiced in the guest house behind the Mansion.

We cut a record at Muscle Shoals, Alabama, called *How Lonesome Can It Be*. It was written by our lead guitarist, Howard DeLorme. I played it for my parents and they really liked it.

The record did very well in Alabama and the surrounding area. It was popular during my mother's fall election campaign. I remember one day all the civics classes at Bellingrath had mock gubernatorial elections, and Mother won in every class by margins of as much as ten to one. In my civics class that day or around that time, some of the students had radios, which were turned on low. And somebody whispered, "Hey—George Jr.'s record is on!"

Our civics teacher, Miss Beckett, said good-naturedly, "Let us hear it!" She was really interested. So someone turned his radio up and the whole class listened to our song. It made me feel like I'd accomplished something.

When my mother won the November election a few days later, everybody congratulated me at school, not only because they were glad she had won, but because they realized that it was unique for a woman to be Governor.

The impact of my mother's victory on my own life really hit me shortly afterward. I was shooting basketballs one day after school when my friend, Coach Charles Lee, the head football coach, came in and said, "Give me a shot." I threw him the ball and gave him a shot, and then he walked by me and said, "How does it feel to have a mother and father as Governor?"

And I told him, "It feels strange!" Because it did. Suddenly I realized that I was the only boy in the country whose parents had both been elected Governor.

C. J. Hartley, who had been so helpful in my mother's campaign, recently told me, "One of the most interesting and rewarding experiences I have ever had was right after the election in 1966, prior to your mother's taking office.

"She called me one day and said, 'I want to get away—there are so many people and all! Can you find a place where I could have a day of relaxation?'

"I've got a little farm, so I said, 'Gosh, yeah! Come on up!' And so she brought her executive secretary from the Mansion along, and her parents, Mr. and Mrs. Burns, and Bobbi Jo and Lee.

"We went down to a little cabin on the place, and spent the entire day. She wanted to get out and fish.

"And then I never will forget, when we finished with lunch she got up and nothin' would do—she had to wash the dishes.

"And she said, 'Now, I want you to put a sign right up over this stove that the Governor washed your dishes!' And I've got a sign in that little camp right now that the Governor washed my dishes.

"But I tell you, to have known that lady was to like her. I mean, she was just a lovely person, and no airs about her. So many people, when they get up the ladder, they start putting on all these fronts. But she never forgot where she came from.

"She was just a very humble person, and I really loved her. And I think the people of Alabama love her today probably equally with Governor George. Because people from all walks of life could go in and talk with her and feel at home, and they can do the same with George."

Although all kinds of people indeed felt at home when they talked to my mother, she herself wanted a place where *she* could feel truly at home—a house of her own, not a Governor's Mansion. So while Dad was still Governor she found a beautiful four-bedroom brick house on Farrar Street in a pleasant residential section of Montgomery, and persuaded my father to purchase it just before she took office.

Dad didn't see why they needed a house right then, since they'd be living in the Mansion for some time, but he bought it to please her. And while Mother was Governor she loved to spend time furnishing the house on Farrar, against the day when she and Dad could move in.

She never did get to live in the house. But the week before she died she visited it one last time to admire some new living room and dining room furniture she'd asked Dad to buy for it. It seemed to be her one hopeful link to a normal life as a housewife in a future she would never see.

By the time she was inaugurated on January 16, 1967, my mother had become an excellent speaker. What she lacked in professional polish she made up in sincerity and heart—especially when she spoke that day of her interest in mental health, a subject close to her heart. Progress in that field would soon become her greatest contribution to the State of Alabama—and her personal memorial.

"I am proud to be an Alabamian," she said in her address. She promised to carry out my father's programs, opposed federal interference in local matters as he had, and said, "I entered the race for Governor for the purpose of permitting my husband to take our fight to the final court of appeal—the people of the United States." And she added, "If there is any change in my administration, it will not be a change of policy or priorities, but rather . . . an attitude reflecting an inner feeling of a wife and mother." That womanly compassion would distinguish her term.

"The mental institutions of our state, overcrowded and understaffed, must receive additional attention," she vowed. It was a promise she would more than keep.

As on the night of her primary victory, she became very emotional at the end of her address, because she was so overwhelmed by the confidence the people had placed in her.

Of course, she knew that *they* knew that my father would be with her in governing the state. But it was still a long way to have come for a country girl from Tuscaloosa who had worked in a dime store after graduating from business school—a *very* long way to the Governorship of Alabama.

Her interest in mental health soon led her back to Tuscaloosa, to tour Bryce State Hospital for the mentally ill and Partlow State School and Hospital for the mentally retarded. And she emerged with tears in her eyes because she was so upset by the plight of the patients, who were terribly overcrowded and without adequate rehabilitation facilities.

She promptly addressed the state legislature on what she had seen—and what must be done to correct such conditions in the state.

Being a compassionate woman, she got upset in that speech. She grew emotional. Tears came to her eyes and her voice broke just thinking about the unfortunate people she had seen at Bryce and Partlow. As a woman, she was uniquely able to show her compassion in this way, and the sincerity of her speech struck a sympathetic chord in the legislature and among the people of the state. She received a standing ovation from the legislators.

In 1967, thanks to my mother's efforts, the state legislature passed a $15,000,000 bond issue to provide mental health and mental retardation reforms. And she signed the legislation into law that September, at a time when she was ill with cancer.

Of course, she also continued many of my dad's programs, as she had promised to do—encouraging industrial development and expanding the interstate highway system, and building more trade schools all over the state. She also continued his program to improve facilities for tuberculosis patients, the program that had been inspired by Uncle Gerald's illness.

Although she was the Governor and my father was her chief adviser, people realized that he was really at the helm, so to speak. But the people's vote of confidence had been in both of them, and her revolutionary mental health program was her own.

She really became involved in running the state—much more than some people had expected. She never was just a pawn in the game. She trusted Dad's judgment, but he listened to her more and more as time went on and she grew more experienced. She studied her job constantly and made a point of familiarizing herself with the legislative process, because she knew how important that was to a Governor, and because she wanted to address the legislature with authority.

She and my father would usually work on these and other speeches together. They shared the same political and governmental philosophy and were partners in every way. But of course, if it came to a decision of great importance as far as the state was concerned, my dad had the dominant voice.

She would seek his advice in most matters, and he in turn would ask her what she thought. It wasn't a case of her just holding the position and his making all the decisions. It was a matter of give and take, and I think it was really a beautiful relationship—the only one of its kind in American history.

Mother dressed neatly but distinctively for the job. She favored colorful blazers with the state seal of Alabama on the breast pocket, and had them in three shades—red, white and blue. With these she would wear double-knit turtlenecks and simple skirts, both in white.

In the day-to-day running of the state, she saw as many visitors in the Governor's office, Room 100, as my father ever had. And he sat in his office across the hall in Room 101 and also saw a steady stream of callers. So each was able to ease the load for the other, really, in handling both official and personal problems for the people who came by.

Often my dad would slip across to her office to confer with her on state business. She learned a great deal about state government in her "on-the-job" training, and with Dad there to advise her she was in no danger of making mistakes because of her newness on the job.

My mother enjoyed being Governor. It was a big responsibility but she realized that and she worked hard at it.

She could also joke about her relationship with my father in his position as her chief adviser.

Col. E. C. Dothard told me that one day there was a cabinet meeting in Mother's office and Dad was a few minutes late. When my father walked into Room 100, Mother and the cabinet were already seated.

She looked up at him and asked with a show of impatience, "Can it wait, George?"

And then she laughed, and everyone else joined in the laughter. She used to kid Dad a lot about things like that, because after all she *was* the *Governor*.

But Dad could kid her, too—as Dave Gardner and his wife, Miss Millie, remember well.

Dave and Miss Millie had invited my parents to attend a Saturday-night show Dave was presenting in Montgomery as part of a tour soon after my mother took office. But my folks had to decline because they were spending many hours on a charity telethon that was running all weekend.

"We stayed over Sunday and went by the Mansion on our way to the airport Monday morning," Dave recalls. "Your folks were there, and Lurleen was all dressed up in her pretty orange suit. You could tell she hadn't had over an hour's sleep, maybe two. Because they had both stayed on right to the end of the telethon. Neither one of them could refuse anything like that.

"So I kissed her on the cheek, and I said, 'That's the first Governor I ever kissed in my life!'"

Miss Millie added, "Then George told Lurleen, 'Well, Honey, go on to the office and run the state.' And she went on out and got in the car, and we said goodbye to her. And we just sat there talking to George."

So if you think my father and mother were like a ventriloquist and his puppet—guess again.

I was very proud of the way she handled her duties as Governor, especially because I knew the problems she'd had about speaking at the beginning of her campaign. And I admired her for being able to get up in front of people and speak well on any occasion. It was a growing process for her. She was coming out. She had been a basically quiet person, not very outgoing but sincere and sympathetic. This was a whole new experience for her, one that taught her a lot about people. And people learned a lot about her. You might say it was an early example of women's liberation, and she handled it tremendously well.

But although she was Governor, she was still my mother. She was the one to whom I instinctively turned after I was involved in a minor auto accident.

I was driving our LTD on a date when I hit a lady's car from behind. She was stopped at a red light and I didn't notice her for some reason, although I was going very slowly.

When she found out who I was, her neck began to hurt her.

We exchanged addresses and license numbers, and I dropped my date off at her house and went home.

My parents were eating when I came in. I went up to Mother and told her what had happened. But it was

Dad who started talking to me about the accident, while I kept talking to Mother about it.

At that point I realized that on matters of that sort I should really be talking to him. And he just took full control. You don't *let* George Wallace take over. He *takes* over. He contacted our insurance company and saw to it that they took care of the matter.

In June, 1967, my mother began to suffer from stomach cramps. Immediately she feared that her cancer had returned.

During a vacation at the Governor's Summer Mansion that June, she told her secretary and confidante, Catherine Steineker, "I won't be here a year from now."

But even when a biopsy at St. Margaret's Hospital later in the month confirmed that another malignancy existed, she maintained a brave front with the family— particularly with my sisters and me. And she kept her fears of death a secret from us not only then but in the painful months that followed. However, before making any public announcement of her condition—usually in connection with an upcoming operation or treatments— she would always tell us first. She didn't want us to get the news from radio or television or the newspapers.

Juanita Halstead believes that hiding her fears from us was made easier for Mother by the fact "that she was not *with* you at that time as much as most mothers are with their children. You were all busy; you were at an age when you were active and doing a lot of things away from her."

This was true. I was busy with my band, although we broke up a few months later when the other members were transferred out of town by the Air Force or left the service. And I was looking forward to entering Sidney Lanier High School for my sophomore year.

Peggy was a camp counselor that summer and was about to start her senior year in high school. Bobbi Jo was married. And little Lee, too young at six to be told much of anything, was at camp with Peggy and had her thoughts on starting the first grade. (Mother took her to school that first day, just as she had done with me.)

But my mother did confide in Juanita. "She was afraid of this disease, this cancer, but it was just something that she knew she had to face," Juanita told me. "And she faced it as bravely as anybody in the world ever *could* face it. But she was still afraid, and I think that's the most normal thing in the world. And she *was* a very *human* person."

When my mother told us that she had cancer again, I didn't for a minute expect she would die. I never thought that until a few days before her death. That's how good a job she did of keeping the seriousness of her condition from her children.

But her doctors wanted her to go to the M. D. Anderson Hospital and Tumor Institute in Houston, Texas, for tests and possible surgery. The hospital is widely renowned for its cancer treatment facilities.

Mother didn't want to leave the state. She preferred to have any further surgery in Alabama, where she could be near the family.

She discussed the matter with my father and her friends. She also sought spiritual guidance from her pastor, the Rev. John Vickers, at St. James Methodist Church.

Finally she agreed to go to Houston. And on June 26, 1967, she made a public announcement to the people of Alabama through her office that "I have a malignancy which may again require surgery. On the recommendation of my doctors . . . I am going to the M. D. Anderson

Hospital in Houston, Texas, for further examination, tests and possible surgery next week."

Peggy, Lee and I told Mother goodbye aboard a private plane at Dannelly Field in Montgomery on July 4, 1967. We would be staying behind, and Mother's parents would be at the Mansion to look after us, as they would have to do several times in the months ahead.

It was a sad moment, yet not without hope. I hated to see her go, but I believed she would be cured in Houston. However, I anxiously checked up on her condition daily while she was in Texas by asking Catherine Steineker about it.

Dad, Bobbi and Mary Jo Ventress accompanied Mother on the flight to Houston, where they stayed at an apartment during her hospitalization and spent as much time with her as possible. She herself stayed at the apartment whenever she could.

On July 10, after several days of tests, the surgeons at M. D. Anderson operated on Mother and removed malignancies from her abdomen and a small cancer from her colon. But they found no other cancer in her body. Again, it was hoped there would not be a recurrence. And she was told immediately after surgery that she would have to return to the hospital for cobalt treatments in September to try to prevent such a recurrence.

Eventually Mother had to make a number of visits to Texas. Among those accompanying her was Colonel Dothard.

"Even when she was *very* sick," he recalled recently, "she never told me how she felt except 'Fine.' I never got any other answer than that, even two days before she died.

"We'd go with her to Texas and we'd rent two apartments out there," he continued. "Security would stay in one, and Governor Lurleen and Governor George or one of her friends would stay in the other. We went to Houston several times. Sometimes it would be for surgery and sometimes for treatment. But she didn't complain."

Mother rested in Montgomery and at Gulf Shores between July twenty-fifth and September tenth, regaining weight and recuperating from her surgery. Then she had to return to Houston for cobalt treatments.

She stayed in Houston until November first, living most of the time at the apartment, since the treatments took only a few minutes a day. She kept in touch with her office by phone. On weekends she would fly home to see us, and always she was reassuring and seemingly confident. We didn't know that the cobalt was causing her increased discomfort and nausea, which sent her to the hospital for a few days in October.

I went to Houston twice to see Mother during her hospitalizations at M. D. Anderson, and the doctors and nurses and hospital personnel all praised her courage and faith.

I learned that she would send most of her flowers to patients who didn't have any, writing an encouraging little note to each. Even when she was so ill, she continued to think of others, and spent much time cheering up the children who were patients at the hospital.

She was always interested in my music. And when I brought a new record of mine to the hospital and played it for her, she insisted on playing it again for the nurses. When the record was played on a Houston radio station, she listened to it with motherly pride.

She was very conscious of her appearance in the hospital. She had brought a large selection of beautiful robe-and-lingerie sets with her so that she would always look her best, and she was careful to have her makeup on when visitors came to call.

When we would see her in the hospital, she would always ask us how *we* were. I think she wanted to turn the attention away from *herself.* And she would always tell us that she loved us. She went through the whole long ordeal with her head high.

I can remember on one trip back from Houston there were four or five thousand people at Montgomery Airport to meet her, and her arrival was televised. She spoke to the crowd from a platform and greeted many of them personally. She'd been in quite a bit of pain on the way back to Montgomery, but in front of the crowd she smiled the whole time.

Mrs. Jack Wise told me, "I never met her at the airport. I always watched her on television. Everybody was waiting for Gov. Lurleen Wallace to come back, and it was televised every time. I have seen her fly in from Houston after having undergone a severe medical treatment, just so bright and happy as she stood and spoke to the people, as though she were going to be here forever. To look at her, you never suspected that Governor Lurleen was ill—at least, not the first time . . . ."

At the time of my mother's illness I was in my sophomore year at Sidney Lanier High School. Upon starting classes there, I had found to my dismay that the school was divided into social groups, and that quite a few students played up to me because of my name. I was too worried about my mother's health to pay much attention to such tactics, but they did result in my becoming more of a loner than I had been in the past.

Midway through the year I started dating a girl named Janice Culbertson, who had just broken up with my friend, Ronnie Wise. I felt she was the *only* girl I could trust. A beautiful brunette and a talented artist, she made it clear that she was interested in *me* and not in my name. We are still going together.

After finishing her cobalt treatments the first of November, Mother drove back to Montgomery with Juanita Halstead instead of flying. She wanted very much to make that beautiful drive through the South, knowing it might be her last. And she bravely insisted on going sightseeing along the way.

That same month she was strong enough to join Dad for appearances in California, where he was signing up voters for his American Independent Party in order to get it on the ballot there during his planned 1968 campaign for President.

At Christmastime she was feeling the dreaded pains again, this time in her lower right side. But she wanted us to have an old-fashioned Christmas as always, so once again she kept the bad news from the family, except for my father, and busied herself buying and wrapping gifts for us all and decorating the Mansion.

Ever since first becoming First Lady, she had extended some of our family Christmas to youngsters in children's homes all over Alabama. She would select and individually wrap between 1,400 and 1,500 little gifts personally, taking months to wrap them at night. They were inexpensive, containing candy or toiletries, but they were greatly appreciated by their recipients.

Even during that last painful December of her life, my mother visited the Methodist Children's Home in Selma, accompanied by Catherine Steineker and the Rev. John Vickers. She made a point of visiting all the cottages and posing for photos with the children—photos which they later received.

With those children, as with her own children at

home in the Mansion, she managed to keep a smile on her face that Christmas season despite the intense pains that were shooting through her.

On January third, the doctors at M. D. Anderson Hospital confirmed the worst: she had another cancer, this time a small pelvic tumor.

My father flew from California, where he had announced that he had obtained enough signatures to qualify for the California ballot, and joined Mother in Houston to comfort her. They returned to Montgomery in separate planes, and Mother made the announcement that she would have to return to Houston in a few days for several weeks of radiation treatments to reduce or, hopefully, remove the tumor.

This time betatron radiation, stronger than cobalt, was used. At first Mother stayed in an apartment again, and Dad remained with her almost constantly to help her endure the agonizing pain of the cancer and the acute discomfort of the treatments.

Somehow Mother managed to make an appearance at the opening of the American Independent Party's Wallace-for-President headquarters in Houston on January eleven.

But when the pain grew too bad at the beginning of February, Mother was admitted to the hospital.

Yet she was determined to return to Montgomery as soon as possible. And on February 4, 1968, having done what they could in the way of treatments, the doctors permitted her to leave Houston and the hospital—for the last time. By now she was being given morphine, a drug she had dreaded taking because of its addictive nature and its associations with terminal cancer.

Mother was at home for less than three weeks in February, resting in bed much of the time but occasionally going for drives and visiting a doctor's office twice weekly for a shot to ease her suffering.

On February twenty-second she was rushed to St. Margaret's Hospital with agonizing intestinal pains. She had a three-hour emergency operation for removal of an intestinal obstruction that had caused the pains. It had been created by the betatron treatments for her pelvic tumor—which was also removed in the surgery and was found to be much shrunken.

I couldn't sleep at the Mansion thinking about my mother alone in the hospital. I felt I had to be with her. So I would go to St. Margaret's to talk to her and would then stay all night in the room outside her hospital room. There were two sofas there where the family could sit.

I would study some and sleep some on the sofa, but I just didn't want to leave. I remember there were certain poems I had to memorize and recite for my sophomore English class at that time, and I learned some of those poems at night in the hospital.

The doctors were optimistic at first because the surgery at St. Margaret's had been a success. But then an abdominal abscess formed, and on March 10 Mother had to have an operation to drain it.

Every one of her four operations, coupled with the radiation treatments, had weakened her, and her recovery was slower this time. But she did improve—until a blood clot formed in her lung toward the end of March. This, too, had to be treated and overcome, and it was.

My father also spent several nights at the hospital with my mother, and saw her daily. They tried to encourage each other, tried to keep hoping. And the Rev. John Vickers was a frequent visitor to the hospital, praying with Mother and offering her spiritual comfort.

She had tremendous religious faith and believed

strongly in an afterlife, and had come to accept the approach of death with increasing calmness—and always with courage despite her very human fears. She secretly discussed funeral arrangements with John Vickers, although we in the family didn't know that until the funeral.

She continued to maintain her surface cheerfulness with her children and friends. "Shortly before Lurleen's death," Mrs. Jack Wise told me, "I was in St. Margaret's Hospital to see a friend. And she said to me, 'Let's go down the hall and see if we can speak to Governor Wallace.' She was Lurleen's neighbor and knew her.

"She and I walked down there, and we saw your father and Bobbi Jo and Mr. and Mrs. Burns. And they, of course, were just hoping and praying, just about as helpless to do anything else as I was.

"But Lurleen was really in good spirits. She didn't want anyone to worry. Peggy went into the room while we were standing outside the door. And she said, 'Peggy, is there something that I can do for you? Is there something you want to know?' She was still trying to do something for people.

"And when you sat up with her at night, she still was not depressing, was she, George? She talked to you as though there'd be much time left."

I agreed, but pointed out, "At that time she was losing a lot of weight, and it really bothered her for someone to see her in that condition. She was always worried about her appearance.

"Daddy took a lot of the pressure off her at that point as far as state affairs," I told Mrs. Wise, as we continued our reminiscences. "He'd bring papers there and discuss them with her at the hospital. Because she *was* still the Governor."

On April 13, 1968, which was Lee's seventh birthday, Mother was allowed to leave St. Margaret's Hospital and return home to the Mansion to continue her hoped-for recovery after nearly two months of hospitalization. Lee had asked her in January, "Mama, will you be home for my birthday?" and Mother had promised to be there.

Peggy had moved out of her room at the Mansion and it had been beautifully redecorated to be Mother's room. (Today Lee lives in it.)

So for the first time Mother and Dad had separate bedrooms—not by choice, but because of the medical equipment she required and the constant day-and-night visits of her nurses to her room. It was Mother's decision to have her own room so as not to disturb Dad.

He took to staying home from the office more and more to be with her as much as possible. And he would still bring her official papers to sign, as if someday she might really return full-time to the Governor's office from which her illness had kept her away so long. Amazingly, Mother continued to ask about some of her pet projects as Governor only a week or two before her death.

Jo Ventress took leave from her job and spent every day with Mother during the final weeks of her life, providing invaluable companionship and a much-needed sense of humor.

We children were going to school, but I took to stopping in to see my mother early in the morning before leaving for class. Each time I went in, I hated to leave. Little Lee watched TV in Mother's room and chatted with her. Peggy also visited Mother frequently and filled her in on her senior class activities at school. Graduation was only a few months away, and Mother gave Peggy her graduation present, diamond earring studs, on the night of Peggy's senior prom. Mary Jo had made Peggy a beautiful pink lace dress for the dance. And Mother even decided on what dress she'd wear to Peggy's graduation. But she knew she might never live that long, and she didn't.

"It was very hard and we were under a lot of pressure," Peggy recalls of those last days in Mother's life. "I just tried to block her illness out of my mind, so that when she did die, it took me a long, long time to accept it."

I, too, never thought of her dying, until almost the very end. She would still take an occasional automobile ride, or sit in the sun in her wheelchair on the patio at the back of the house. Drugs eased much of her pain.

I remember during those last few weeks at the Mansion I got upset with my mother a little, because the nurse had told me she wouldn't eat. She had no appetite at all, and had lost almost 30 pounds at that point from her regular weight of 105.

I had started working out at a health spa and eating a lot of this, that and the other, and when her tray was brought to her I exclaimed, "Mother, just—*eat* it. Just—*make* yourself eat it!"

And she looked up at me and said, in a voice that had become pitifully weak, "Son, I would if I could."

By now she didn't even have the strength to hide her condition from us. She was terribly frail, and her face was thin and gaunt as the disease took its toll. Yet she never complained, and we didn't allow ourselves to think the end was near, even though it hurt us so much to see her that way.

One day I went into her room at the Mansion and found her knitting, as she often did to pass the time. She looked up and said she had something for me.

And she brought out a beautiful Bible and gave it to

me. I opened it, and inside were written the words, "To our son with love and affection," with her name and Dad's name and the date.

Another blood clot formed at the beginning of May, six days before my mother's death, and hastened the end of her life. Although nobody knew it at the time, her cancer had spread by now to her liver and lungs. As her pain increased, the doctors gave her more medication—a morphine derivative.

She told my father that she was afraid the end was near. And he, too, feared the worst. But he tried to reassure her, and she promised him that she would try as best she could to hold onto life. Yet she was steadily weakening.

Dad came into my room one night shortly afterward and I asked, "Dad, how's Mother?"

And he said quietly, "Well, Son, your mother may not *make* it." I remember that very vividly and always will, for that's the first time it really struck me that she might *not* make it.

I became very upset, and when he had left the room I started crying. That night I couldn't sleep.

I talked to my mother for the last time on May sixth, the day before she died. I could see that she was in great pain. All I could say was, "Mother, how do you feel?" And even then, hours away from death, she just smiled and didn't complain. Yet I could tell that she couldn't bear for me to see her suffering so.

Her pain worsened through the day, yet as each of her children came in to see her, she would smile once again. But with my father and Mary Jo Ventress, and with the nurses and doctors, she was candid about the pain and her fear that death was not far off.

By nightfall, all the members of the family had gathered at the Mansion to await the end: Dad, all the children, Mother's parents, and her brother and sister-in-law. Mother went into a coma about two hours before she died.

"They called me from play practice over at my high school," Peggy Sue remembered recently, "and I came over here to the Mansion. I think you were in my bedroom with me."

I nodded. "At one point I think I *was* in your room. Then we were all out in the hallway, where we had the sofa."

Peggy said, "I can remember Dr. (H. H.) Hutchinson coming into the hallway and saying, 'About fifteen minutes.' And then he'd come back and say, 'Maybe ten.' And it never hit me, you know, that he was really saying it!"

We were all together in Mother's room a few minutes before she died. It was a beautiful room, decorated in shades of turquoise and touches of green, but it had seen so much suffering the past few weeks.

Now my mother, her weight reduced to sixty-eight pounds by disease, was about to be released from all her pain. Her eyes were closed, and she was breathing deeply —long, long breaths.

Dad held her hand and named all of us who were gathered in the room, and he told Mother how much we all loved her.

Then he asked her to squeeze his hand if she could hear him. And she *did* squeeze his hand. She understood.

She continued to grasp Dad's hand as her breaths became shorter, and gradually her grip weakened.

Dad asked Dr. Hutchinson, "Is she gone?"

Dr. Hutchinson did not reply. He put his stethoscope to Mother's chest, and when he felt no heartbeat he simply took the stethoscope off his ears in a weary gesture of defeat that said it all.

The time was 12:34 A.M. Tuesday, May 7, 1968.

Chapter Nine

MOTHER had discussed the possibility of her dying with her close friends and my father. And although she didn't reveal to them that she had already planned out her funeral with the Rev. John Vickers, she did tell them that she didn't want her casket to be open, because she had lost so much weight.

But my dad decided to open it, because although she was very thin she still looked like herself.

Dad discussed the question with me before making his decision, and I wanted the people to see her. I agreed with him completely.

So Mother's body lay in state in an open coffin, in the rotunda of the Capitol, on the spot where a beautiful white marble bust of her stands today. On the pedestal are the words from her inaugural address: "I am proud to be an Alabamian."

The family accompanied her body to the Capitol. I remember I held my dad's hand in the car on the way up to the Capitol and back, and I would squeeze it to keep from crying. He managed to keep his emotions in. He was very quiet that day, but I could tell he really missed Mother. I cried a little in the Capitol, but I knew she wouldn't have wanted us to.

We stayed in the Capitol rotunda while they opened Mother's coffin and held a brief memorial service. Then we left her to the people of Alabama, who came through by the thousands, registering their grief and their love by weeping openly as they passed the coffin, many of them commenting on what a great lady she had been.

The Mansion seemed so empty and lonely without Mother that I went to stay for a few days with my friend, Ronnie Wise, and his parents, at my "second home."

Ronnie's mother, Mrs. Jack Wise, recalled, "When Lurleen's body was lying in state at the Capitol, you could not get near! I stood in line for three or four hours with the children, and finally I told a policeman, 'I have left little George at my home, and please just let me come up.' Of course, I was trying for privilege for myself, which I don't suppose I should have.

"The policeman said, 'Well, why didn't you *bring* George?' I said, 'I don't know. I just left him at my home.' Now, I doubt if he even believed what I said, you know?

"But anyway, we returned home—never even did get *near* Dexter Avenue. They had stopped all the traffic in every direction. And this went on all through the night, until morning, didn't it, George?

"I remember when I got home I told you, 'George, I did not get to pass by your mother and pay my respects.' And you said, 'Well, Mrs. Wise, I'll go with you tonight.' But it was about dark when I got home, and of course I didn't let you *do* this, because you'd had about all you could withstand.

"But to my mind you handled yourself beautifully," she added. "You were very pleasant around the house, and you ate real good. You didn't have too much to say, but you seemed *very* well adjusted and well prepared. I thought you really showed great strength."

I replied, "I think some of the family strength came from my mother. There in the last few days we saw *her* strength."

Peggy Sue remembers, "The day of the funeral they carried the casket out of the Capitol and brought it to the Mansion to lie in state over here. On the way, you were in the car with Daddy and me. And I just remember crying out loud all of a sudden. And you put your arm around me.

"And I remember thinking, 'Oh, how I wish we could always be as close as this.' And I think we *have* been since then. I think we're still getting that way, because we used to not be close at all. We used to really never care about each other until Mother died.

"You went your way and I went mine, and what you did didn't interest me. And what I did *definitely* didn't interest *you!*" she continued, adding:

"I'm a very emotional person and you are not. I can *never* remember you being emotional about Mother's death. Never! I just would cry for days, but you never showed any emotion at *all* that I can remember.

"You're very—deep. You have a very mature way of getting rid of your anxiety and emotions, you really do. I tried to figure you out, and I'm going to one of these days!" she smiled.

And yet it was hard for *any* of us to control our emotions at the funeral. Lee in particular was very upset. She was very young, and we had spared her from attending most of the memorial observances. But at the funeral, Dad was holding her and she was crying. Bobbi cried a little, although she tried to hold it back. Peggy was as upset as she could be, and so was I, even though I kept my composure.

"At that age, it would have been really detrimental to Lee if they had let her go through all the lying-in-state and going to the funeral home and all the things that we had to do," Peggy believes. "It seems like it lasted a week! It was all very long and drawn out.

"For the family all the ceremonies were just something you had to go through. When a state official passed on, it was just something you had to do.

"But as for Lee, they'd say, 'Spare her this,' because she was only seven years old, and she didn't understand. And as she has grown older she doesn't have that many memories."

The Rev. John Vickers, Mother's very close friend and our pastor, conducted the funeral, which was held May 9, 1968, at St. James Methodist Church, where Mother had loved to worship.

In addition to my father, my sisters and myself, Mother's parents and other relatives and countless friends were there, including many state officials. The church was packed.

As part of the service, music selected by Mother was played, and John Vickers read two poems that Mother had requested: an inspirational poem entitled *I Love You,* and, especially for the members of the family, Elizabeth Barrett Browning's immortal poem which begins, "How do I love thee? Let me count the ways," and ends, "and, if God choose, I shall but love thee better after death."

Mother was buried in Montgomery's Greenwood

Cemetery, and today her burial place has a beautiful marble monument in a circle with a flag in the center. It has been named the Governors' Circle, with the thought that other Governors of Alabama may wish to be buried there in the future. And of course Dad will be buried by Mother's side. The monument simply lists her name and title, Gov. Lurleen Burns Wallace, the dates she served as Governor, and the dates of her birth and death. All of us in the family visit the grave frequently, particularly at Christmas, Thanksgiving and Mother's birthday, September nineteenth.

I think Mother does know how very much everyone in the family misses her. Life has never been the same since she died.

"It's just that she cared so much for us," Peggy Sue observed, "and as we've grown older we've realized that more and more.

"She died when we were at an age where we needed a mother most—I was 18, and you were 16—and an age when children are most rebellious," Peggy Sue added. "So I think we missed that stage of our growing up. I don't think we had a *chance* to rebel against our parents, because she was sick so long and died such a slow death."

Come to think of it, there's a lot of truth in what Peggy said. Neither of us ever *was* a rebellious teen-ager. Some people may think that was all to the good, but it was a part of life that we missed out on, in any case.

I was out of school for a couple of days after Mother's funeral, and when I returned all the students and teachers were very nice to me. They knew how close Mother and I had been.

Lt. Gov. Albert Brewer had automatically become

Governor upon Mother's death, and he assured the family that we could take a good length of time in moving out of the Mansion—as long as we wanted. But my dad, of course, said we'd move right out, and we did, a few days after Mother was buried.

We moved to the house on Farrar Avenue that she had picked out and furnished. It was waiting there for us, as though Mother had known we'd need it.

"The family pulled closer together after Mother's death," Peggy Sue recalls. "It was a case of having to do it or else.

"And we had to be closer for Daddy's sake," she added. "He was such a heartbroken man—few people can imagine how heartbroken he *was*.

"With only you and little Lee and me at home with Daddy, I had to play Mother. And Daddy was so heartbroken that *he* really couldn't play any role at all! So it was left up to *all* of us to become closer, and I think we did. We just *had* to. It wasn't like it just grew gradually. We had to do it just like *that!*" And she snapped her fingers.

"But Daddy was in that depressed mood for months and months and months," Peggy recalled. "I think his politics probably was the best cure for that. It got him back into the swing of things.

"I can remember one time—I don't think you were there, George—I can remember Daddy and I just lying on the couch and crying together. And I remember thinking *then,* too, as I had with you in the car, that I wished we could always be close like that."

When he could pull himself together, Dad began working daily, on a year-around basis, at his national campaign headquarters, which were located in the Lowder Building in Montgomery. He had his office there until he became Governor again in 1971.

Two of the security men who had been with him resigned from the state troopers to come with him after he left the Mansion, because they loved my dad and believed in him that much. They guarded his office and our home.

At that point I can remember my dad and I spent more time together. Of course we'd eat together every day —Eloise had come with us to cook and take care of the house and look after Lee—and the house was more like a home than the Mansion had ever been, except that we missed Mother so. I'd see him more because he wasn't as busy as he had been when he was Governor or acting as Mother's chief adviser.

Even though he would go to work at the national campaign headquarters daily, sometimes he would leave there early. He would come out to the house in the afternoon when I was home from school, and he would say, "Son, let's go for a ride." He had a 1968 LTD, and we would go—and he would *drive,* for the first time in years.

I can remember from my earlier days, he used to scare my mother when he would drive. He was a good driver but sometimes he didn't *concentrate* on his driving. He'd pass a car in a curve, and I could see my mother getting upset. But he would slip back in. He just wasn't conscious of driving. His mind was on other things.

But after we moved out of the Mansion it really made me feel good to be riding with him. I'd never seen him drive that much. And there was no security man with us—just my dad and me! They would go home at night, except for one man at the back door of the house.

We'd drive down the Southern Bypass, a four-lane

highway which bypasses the city, and sometimes we'd just drive through Montgomery. And it would shock people when he'd pull up to a red light. They would look over and see him, and he would smile and wave. And the people would wave back and punch their friends in the car and say, "That's Governor Wallace!"

I remember we would ride along and he would say, "Son, I really miss your mother." Of course, I knew that. *Everyone* knew that. And as we drove along he said on a couple of occasions how much the people of the state loved and admired her, and that she was really someone to be proud of. I think he spent more time with us because he did miss her so much, and we brought him closer to her.

Yes, I really enjoyed those drives with my father, but I don't think *he* realized how much they meant to me. When he'd say, "Come on, Son, let's go for a ride," that was really something for me. Usually in a father-and-son relationship it's very common, I guess. But for *me* it wasn't. It *never* was! This was the first time in years we'd had a normal life.

Of course, in one tragic way it *wasn't* normal. For the first time my dad was thrown into the situation where he was the only parent. And that's probably a difficult situation for *any* parent. As Peggy said, for a while he couldn't fill the role because of his grief.

But as time passed, we could go to him with our problems. I know *I* did. I tried not to have too many problems that I couldn't handle myself, however. Because we were the only two men in the house, so to speak, and I felt I should be more independent at that age, and that I should help look after the girls.

Lee, being the youngest child, took Mother's loss the hardest. We tried to spend extra time with her, but there's only so much you can do to comfort someone. However, Lee was very proud of Mother then and she is now. She's very much like her in personality—lively and humorous— and she even *looks* like her. I notice that as she gets older.

Eventually, we made some friends down the street, and that was good for Lee, I think, because it was a nice area, and in the Mansion she hadn't been able to meet other children as easily as she did now. She got a trampoline, and at one point she had a monkey in a cage in the backyard. My dad named him Claude—after a certain political rival, some people said!

I had my guitar and amplifier in my room, and my stereo between the two beds. Dad's room was at the back of the house. He had his bedroom, and from there you walked through a door into his study.

My room was by his, and to get to his room he had to walk by mine. Consequently he would knock on my door most of the time when he'd go by, and I was able to see even more of him that way. So all in all we were much closer than we had been before.

I was with another band for a short time in 1968. There were five of us in it—the others were older students. And for the first time I wasn't just singing. The bass player handled most of the vocal chores. I was playing lead guitar, and I really enjoyed it. I felt I was contributing more to the group by playing.

We performed at service clubs at Guntar Air Force Base and Maxwell Air Force Base, which are on opposite sides of Montgomery, and we appeared at other places, too. I remember an amusing incident at Wetumpka, a small town about fifteen miles north of Montgomery, where we played at a teen dance. People there knew who I was.

Whenever you play these places, you notice that if the girls who come with dates start looking at the guys in your group like they dig them, their dates take it out on the band members. It happened to me in Wetumpka. And all I was doing was sitting there pickin'.

During a break I had to go out and move my car because a policeman said it was in the wrong spot. And when I went out to move it, there were about twelve guys sitting on my car—twelve!

I said, "Hey, guys, they told me I should move my car around the block. Y'all want to hop off and let me move it?" And every one of them gave me looks which said they weren't moving.

So I just smiled at them and turned around and walked back in. I told the policeman I thought I was going to have some trouble moving my car—because I was!—so he helped me get it moved.

Not long after that incident, the band broke up, but I learned a lot about music playing with that group. It was a valuable experience.

Now that I was in high school, Dad and I had some father-son disagreements. My father worried about me, because in high school students become more aware of drinking. And there was a lot of it going on at the ball games. I gave him no particular reason to be concerned, but just as a father he was afraid that I might get mixed up with some of the wrong people and start drinking and have a car wreck or something. So he would lecture me.

In high school I did drink occasionally, but I didn't particularly care for it that much. So I would tell him that he didn't have to worry about that.

Of course, since he doesn't drink himself, he was really against alcohol, and I realized it. But I made up my own mind as far as drinking. I didn't let his feeling about alcohol influence *me*. It was just that I had tried it and didn't especially like it.

But I was into cars. I had a 1968 yellow Chevelle with a 396 cubic-inch engine, four-speed with a tach. (It was the car so many people sat on in Wetumpka.) My friends and I took the engine out of that car and put it in a 1968 Nova, very light. And we put a 410 rear end in it, which is good for the quarter mile. We dragged it at the drag strip in Montgomery, which was sanctioned and had special lights. We didn't drag on the street.

I enjoyed racing, and I won some races and lost others. I wasn't playing music at that point, except to practice at home. So I didn't have any income from music. But my friends would help me if they'd get some money and we needed something like tires for the car.

I can't remember ever getting a set allowance. If I needed some money, my dad would help me. But I can say he really didn't understand my interest in cars, because *he'd* never been interested in them, since from the age of fifteen he'd wanted to be Governor.

He was starting to see that our interests were different, and I think it took as much adjusting for him as it did for me. Because he'd had quite an influence on me while I was growing up; I could see what he'd done and what he was accomplishing. But now I was starting to branch out on my own.

However, I hadn't yet decided during my high school days to be a musician. I was thinking of being a lawyer like Dad. But I couldn't develop any interest in it. I was *thinking* that was what I should do because people thought I should do it: I've seen a lot of people around my dad who really can't understand to this day why I decided to go into music. They don't really approve. But it's not for them to say, or understand my music.

I traveled with my father everywhere he went during the Presidential campaign of 1968. We had our own campaign plane, a large four-engine propeller-driven model. I only played at his rallies a couple of times that year. Mostly I was along to keep him company, because he was still depressed over Mother's death, as I was. I would sit beside him on the plane.

It was a strenuous campaign, and he was tired a lot of the time. So he was pretty quiet on the plane. At my age—I was sixteen—there was no way I could really get into his world or offer any suggestions on his campaign. I wasn't experienced enough. But he knew I was there, and that was what mattered.

I can read his moods pretty well, and I tried to adhere to them on the plane. If he was in a talkative mood, I'd talk with him. He might ask me what I thought about the traveling, the places we'd been, and I'd tell him. If he was quiet and wanted to think, I'd be satisfied to sit by him.

Of course, he flew in a bomber in World War II, so he knew the sounds of the engines very well. He could tell if something wasn't quite right. And one time as we were taking off he said, "One of the engines on the left doesn't sound right." Sure enough, the pilot came on the intercom and said we were going to land—that one of the engines was malfunctioning. Dad had heard it before any of *us* knew it. We couldn't tell. Fortunately we had no trouble landing.

Dad is very cautious about flying. He doesn't like to fly unless it's very good weather. He doesn't like to fly at night. Of course, he *will*, but he asks and asks the proper people if it's all right to fly, and they always reassure him.

The Presidential campaign of 1968 was pretty hostile in places. It had been only five years since Dad's school-house-door stand, and people remembered that.

Gen. Curtis LeMay, his running mate on the American Independent Party ticket, was a very impressive man who had quite a bit of trouble with the press. He didn't exactly know how to handle reporters and they would turn around what he said, or get him excited and angry and make him say what they wanted to hear. I think my dad helped him regarding how to deal with the press. There's an art to it.

I really enjoyed campaigning that year. I had a chance to see a lot of the country and meet many people, and I realized more than ever just how popular Dad was outside the state. Of course, Alabama went strongly for him, and almost everyone I knew was on his side. But to see his national impact was reassuring.

However, that was the first year I personally had a good chance to see the people who were against him—the people who heckled him or tried to stop him from finishing his speeches. And I think they bothered me more then than they did in 1972, because it was so new to me.

But as usual it didn't affect Dad. He knew how to handle hecklers. He would never get excited, never lose his temper. If he could get them to listen, that's what he tried to do. He didn't consider them his enemies although *they* felt that way about *him*. And if trouble ever broke out during a speech, Dad would always tell his supporters, "Let the police handle it."

There were some surprisingly nice moments. Once a girl with sandals and long hair—people would have called her a hippie in those days—had some flowers. And she indicated to Dad that she wanted to bring the flowers up on the stage. I think she thought he'd be offended. But he motioned for her to come up, and smiled and took the flowers. And she wanted to kiss him. So he bent down and she kissed him on the cheek. That surprised some of the people who were against him, and they applauded him.

Dad received ten million votes in 1968 as the candidate of the American Independent Party. He won 45 electoral votes and carried five states, showing his was a movement to be reckoned with in the future. And of course it originated in Alabama, giving the people of our state a hearing all across the nation through him.

For my part, in the 1968 campaign I began to see more clearly what Dad is trying to do, and I realize it more fully every day. He's one of the few, if not the only one, who hasn't sold out. He's his own man. It's the little people, the average citizens, who contribute to his campaigns. I think he said they've had some $5,000 contributions from staunch supporters, but he owes no favors because of big money.

He's still talking against the federal government's encroachment on local institutions because that issue hasn't been resolved yet. That's why he has been against school busing.

And in 1968 he especially spoke out for law and order. A lot of the liberal press tried to make something of that, as though it were a code phrase for being antiblack. But he simply meant being able to walk down the street in your city without fear of getting hit on the head, and before they get you to the hospital the person who hit you is out of jail, and next day they try the policeman. That's an exaggeration, but he's talking about *everyone's* safety when he talks about law and order.

And as I've said, it was in 1968 that I became more

concerned about Dad's own safety, after Martin Luther King and Robert Kennedy were killed. I especially worried when he went out into the crowds.

I became very good friends with many of the Secret Service men assigned to his detail, and they were very competent people. But I realized there's only so much the Secret Service can do. They can't guarantee that someone won't get to you—if he really wants to.

Chapter Ten

ALTHOUGH 1969 was not an election year, I continued to work for my father's campaign that spring—in the mailroom of his national campaign headquarters.

I picked up and carried the mail, and sent out packages and literature. Dad continued to be very popular all over the nation, and people were writing in for Wallace-for-President publications and pictures, pins and bumper stickers. There were even license plate holders that read "Wallace Country."

I was paid the same hourly wage as everyone else for my part-time job—about $1.60 an hour. There wasn't a lot of money available, and the people who worked at Dad's headquarters did so because they were really involved. That's still true.

But even in Alabama, of course, my father had his detractors, as he does today. Once when I was in high school I found myself defending him not only verbally but physically.

It happened at a party. An Air Force man was there, and he'd had a little too much to drink. And he found out who I was.

I went out to the kitchen to get something, and when I came back I passed by his chair. Suddenly he called Dad a dirty name.

I just turned around and knocked him out of the chair. The chair turned over with a clatter and he was on the floor.

He jumped up, and we went outside on the balcony to have it out. He knocked me down. Then I got up and knocked *him* down again, and they had to pull me off him, because he was almost unconscious by then.

I never had been that mad before, and it really surprised me. But when I heard him say, "Your dad's a such-and-such," it was just more than I could take. I shouldn't have done it, really, but sometimes you can't stay away from those things.

He did apologize later that night, and I said, "Yeah, well, just forget it," and turned away from him. I was with some friends and we left the party. He had pushed too far and paid the price, and I didn't want to stand around saying, "We're friends."

Those things, as I say, are going to happen. When you're in public life and as controversial as my dad, it's going to affect your family. It's *got* to.

In my senior year at Sidney Lanier High School, the students were still very social-minded, but I wasn't really into any social cliques. I just went to school, made my grades, and that was it.

I had the feeling that some people thought that by being who I was I should stand out more or something. But that wasn't me. I enjoyed school, but as far as the social scene I just didn't fit in. It all seemed ridiculous to me.

I saw a lot of people in high school who were trying to impress others with stylish clothes, money or social standing. But I never was like that and I never wanted to impress people that way. If I wanted to impress anyone at all, I wanted to do it just by being myself. I suppose that's a heritage from my mother and father, neither of whom had ever been interested in "crashing society."

Growing up as I did, in a political atmosphere, I saw a lot of phonies around my dad at one time or another. They were the kind who'll hang around *any* politician.

The people around Dad generally are real people, because he's an excellent judge of character and he knows where a person's head is. But there have been some who've been around him now and then, down through the years, who were there for their personal gain. That was as far as they could see. The good of this country and the goals my father has had were things they could never see because of their own personal ambitions.

Although I always avoided phonies in high school, luckily I did have some good friends I hung around with. And I had my girl friend, Janice Culbertson.

She and I went to high school football games together, and to movies. But mostly I would just go over to her house and visit. Her parents and I have always gotten along very well—her father is an executive for Frito-Lay— and I'm also close to her sister, Donna.

How did I know that Janice accepted me for myself and not for my name? It's something you can't fully explain—just a question of chemistry. But for one thing, she never sought to meet me as some girls did. As I said, she had previously dated my good friend, Ronnie Wise. And

I would discuss their problems with her, because they were having arguments as their romance broke up. So we became interested in each other gradually, with no pressure on either side. It was all very natural and honest. In addition, she was deeply involved with her interest in painting, so that she avoided the social scene just as I did.

I continued to cherish the times I could spend with my father, and to be grateful that we were seeing more of each other than when he was in office.

I can remember just before he ran for Governor in 1970, we were in Panama City together, in northern Florida. He has a friend who has a place there and we were staying with him.

I could see, as I had before, that he relaxes in his own way. If he's around a newspaper he'll always be reading it. And it's the same way with a book. He enjoys reading books about politics, histories and biographies.

He's never given me a lot of father-and-son advice. He never told me about the "facts of life." Mainly he just told me to study hard, and of course he's always wanted me to finish school.

Sometimes he consciously avoids giving me advice, even when he sees something's wrong, preferring to let me work things out so that I'll learn from experience.

For instance, not long ago I had a group of musicians that I got together in Montgomery. And we had some problems, because these fellows weren't really into my music. It was like they were using me—using my name— for their own gain.

And so the group didn't work out. And later, after it was over, Dad told me, "Son, I saw that all the time. And I'm glad you realize it now." Others had warned me we'd have problems, but my father never had.

He could easily have told me, since he's such an astute judge of character, but he was glad I found it out for myself. I think that's the best way, really.

I asked him one time if he could walk into a room full of people and tell who was for him and who was against him politically. And he said he could. I believe he can tell it immediately by observing people's reactions. Good politicians can do that. And I wish *I* could do it.

In the 1970 primary, Dad ran against the incumbent, Albert Brewer, for the Governorship. (The gubernatorial succession law had been repealed in 1968 by vote of the legislature and the people, but that did not affect my father's 1970 candidacy anyway, because he was not running for a second consecutive term that year—although it did permit him to run to succeed himself in 1974.)

I had known Governor Brewer and his daughters, Becky and Alison, and he had been friends with my parents. When he ran for Lieutenant Governor in 1966, the year my mother ran for Governor, they were not paired on the ticket, as it isn't done that way in Alabama. But Mother and Dad favored his candidacy. He had been Speaker of the Alabama House of Representatives.

But sometimes politics can interfere with friendships. One of my best friends at school, Dickie Whitaker, who became my roommate at the university after the 1970 election, had been assistant reading clerk in the House and worked very hard for Brewer when he was Speaker.

So when Dad and Governor Brewer ran against each other in 1970, it was a trying time for Dickie—because he was my close friend, he was for my dad, and yet he was friends with many of Governor Brewer's supporters and with the Governor himself. I'm sure he was glad when the election was over and done with.

I've been asked whether the rivalry between Governor Brewer and my father in 1970 was just a political rivalry or was it personal bitterness.

As far as my dad was concerned, it was a political rivalry. But I think some of the people in both camps took it personally. It was a very hot political race—a very *close* political race.

I traveled across the state with Dad in the 1970 campaign, singing and playing my guitar at his rallies. There were several country artists appearing on the program with us. He had Jeannie C. Riley and the Logan Brothers, and Roy Clark of TV's *Hee Haw* was with him a couple of times. I got to know Roy pretty well, and he's a really nice man and a talented entertainer. I think working with these people inspired me, and I enjoyed the experience.

But the campaign had its unpleasant moments. During that election Dad went to the University of Alabama to give a speech at the invitation of a group called Emphasis 70, which brought in various speakers. He had done more for that school, his alma mater, than had any other Governor, generously providing funds and facilities for it. Yet he was booed by half the audience—students who were sitting down front and wouldn't let him be heard.

These students were supposed to be so open-minded, and they were always talking about freedom of speech and the rights of the individual. But yet they wouldn't listen to my father speak.

Well, those students didn't realize that politically that was the best shot in the arm he could have had in Alabama.

I believe Dad knew what was going to happen before he went, because he's very astute politically. So he used that incident to his advantage. The average man in

Alabama watching it on television, seeing what was happening at the institution he was supporting with his taxes, didn't like what he saw. So it helped Dad with the voters.

I think the colleges have calmed down now, with students more work-conscious and more interested in learning and getting ahead. They're still concerned with politics, as they should be, but they don't lean toward violence and disorder any more as they used to. I know that from my own experience as a college student at the present time.

I think you should go to college to prepare yourself professionally and broaden yourself intellectually, and then get out in the real world, where you can see what it's really like.

That student newspaper at the university, the *Crimson and White*—it's never been very kind to Dad. Well, you get ten miles out of town and nobody knows what the *Crimson and White* is. Life isn't on a college campus. It's working and providing for your family and paying taxes. We don't live in a utopia and never will. So you have to work within the political system and *listen* to people and decide for yourself by exercising your right to vote, rather than shouting people down.

Of course, we have the right to dissent, but to deprive someone else of his freedom to speak is wrong.

My dad has a lot of faith in young people, though. He really does. He *loves* young people. And I wish they could be more open-minded about him as a person, because he's very open-minded about them.

If they would look at some of the programs he's initiated—the junior colleges, the trade schools, the hospitals, the highway system—they might agree with my own feeling that history will be very kind to him.

The Watergate investigations have since brought out that $4oo,ooo came to Dad's opponent, Governor Brewer, in 1970 from national Republican sources on a secret basis. During that time my father was saying, "Big money's coming in." He didn't have any details, but *he* knew it was coming in. He knew they were out to get him—to stop him. He could see it in his opponent's spending, because he's always keenly aware of what goes on in a campaign.

Apparently the aim behind that $400,000 was to destroy my dad as a potential presidential rival to President Nixon in the 1972 election, because in 1968 his American Independent Party candidacy, by making it a three-way race, had resulted in an extremely close contest between President Nixon and Sen. Hubert Humphrey. If the people of your home state reject you as a candidate for Governor, you're pretty well washed up nationally.

Another thing Governor Brewer had going for him was the power of being the incumbent. In *any* state the incumbent Governor has a lot of power, because he can dole out favors and make appointments, and this can influence political support.

I wasn't too knowledgeable about that sort of thing, but I remember asking my dad early in the campaign, "How do you think it's going to go?"

And he said: "Son, it's going to be a tough race." He added that he might even run behind in the first primary.

I really hadn't expected him to say anything like that. I thought he was just being overly cautious, because I was always sure he would win.

And then I saw what he was talking about. It *was* a tough race. He knew it all the time. It happened exactly the way he said it was going to happen.

Naturally much of the press was against him as usual. I can remember a friend of mine drove me to Tuscaloosa one weekend. Governor Brewer was speaking in Tuscaloosa that night.

We heard on the car radio that the Governor had five or six thousand people at his rally, and how enthusiastic they were—how well he was received, and what a great speech he was making.

We decided to drive to the rally, and when we arrived there were maybe a thousand people present.

It was really amusing to me, because Daddy never had any trouble drawing a crowd.

However, in the first primary Governor Brewer came in first, and Dad was in second place. So they were forced into a runoff, because nobody had won more than half the votes.

The night he came in second in the primary, Dad took it very coolly. He knew he had a hard job to do if he was to turn the election around. And he worked harder than ever from then on, campaigning and registering voters.

Dad managed to pull victory out of defeat and won the runoff by over 35,000 votes. On the night of his runoff victory, I went to his campaign headquarters instead of to my own graduation from Sidney Lanier High School.

Everyone at the headquarters was really just ecstatic, because they had all worked so hard for my father's election. And Dad was really happy.

Dad easily won the November election and another term as Governor. By then I was a business and commerce student at the University of Alabama.

I knew how the college students had treated Dad when he spoke there, so I expected the experience to be interesting—and it was. I met new friends, as I knew I would. And I met some people who were very small-minded. Because they didn't agree with my dad politically, right away they formed an opinion that they didn't like *me*.

They wouldn't tell me so to my face, but when someone in the room is cold to me I not only can sense it right away, I can then ignore him completely. And in a little while it's as though he isn't even there. I let him play his game within his own head, which puts *him* down, not me.

Some people did criticize Dad to my face at the university, but I didn't mind that. Because I knew they were talking about him in a political vein, not personally. He's taken a lot of abuse, so *I* can take a little abuse.

I had started at the university during the summer session, to have a head start. And I was going through some mental adjustments aside from the natural ones of leaving your family to live in a campus atmosphere.

I had become accustomed to living in our house on Farrar, which had been so much more of a home than the Mansion ever was. It didn't have houses for security people and it didn't have tourists coming through. Now I realized that I'd soon be spending weekends and vacations at the Mansion again, with all that it involved.

And more importantly, I would be seeing much less of my father than I had during the past two years. Not only distance but time would be separating us—the time he would once more be giving to his duties as Governor. I realized nothing would ever be quite the same again.

I was interested in a fraternity, Pi Kappa Phi, when I first went to the university during the summer session, and was happy to realize that the majority of the fellows were not interested in my name but wanted me to offer the group something like everybody else, and wanted to offer

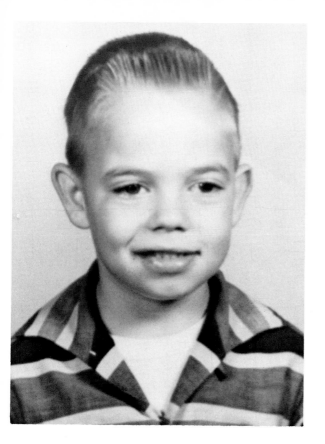

I was born October 17, 1951, in Clayton, Alabama, where we lived while Dad was a member of the Alabama state legislature. In 1952 he was elected circuit judge of Alabama's Third Judicial District. I remember visiting Dad's office in the courthouse and sitting behind his big wooden desk. This picture of Peggy Sue and myself (above, right) was taken just down the street from the courthouse where Dad used to sit out on a bench and chat with the citizens of Barbour County. In the photo above I was in the first grade and here (at right) are Bobbi Jo, Peggy Sue (to my right) and one of our friends on a trip we took to Florida about 1956.

Unless otherwise credited, these photos are from the Wallaces' family album.

One day Dad came home and talked excitedly with Mother in the den. I knew that something big was going on, but I was only six years old and I couldn't figure it out. When I asked her, she told me, "Your daddy's going to run for Governor." At first I didn't know what that meant, but as the campaign picked up momentum I began to understand. I memorized a little page-and-a-half speech and I traveled around giving it for Dad. Here's our family—Dad, me, Mom, Bobbi Jo and Peggy Sue—at a televised kickoff for Dad's 1958 campaign (above). Here he is at a campaign rally (right) and on the stump in Alabama (opposite, top).

I got to pose with Curley Brooks (with the bass) and one of the bands that traveled with Dad (opposite). Curley also traveled with Dad in 1968. Here we are at a hotel in Montgomery where Dad was speaking (right). Dad went into a runoff with Jim Patterson that year, and Patterson won. Dad was disappointed, I guess, but I think he mostly saw 1958 as a prelude to 1962.

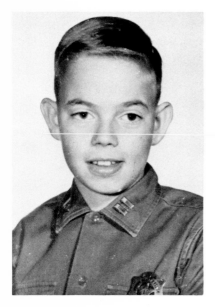

In 1961 we moved to a cramped little apartment in Montgomery, and Dad started to work on his next campaign for Governor. Mother and Dad traveled across the state, though Lee was just a baby. She was born in 1961, just before we moved to Montgomery. Dad won the primary, and the election. His inauguration was on January 19, 1963, one of the coldest days of the year. It was a very formal affair, with all the men wearing top hats and morning coats. I was only eleven years old, but I was also dressed in formal attire. I stood with Peggy (left), my mother and Bobbi Jo to have our picture taken at the Mansion before going to the parade (above). Here is Dad with Mother and Oscar Harper, a longtime friend at the leadoff for the first dance at the ball (above, left).

Life at the Mansion was exciting and a big change for us, but we all gradually adjusted and learned to love it. I was in the sixth grade when we moved in (opposite) and captain of the patrol boys at school. I had a horse for awhile and these pictures were taken at a horse show in Millbrook where I showed in the Western Class in 1964.

By the summer of 1963, I was aware of many of my father's achievements as Governor, but I was also aware that he was pretty controversial. That summer he became even more controversial, standing dramatically "in the schoolhouse door" at the University of Alabama denying Assistant Attorney General Nicholas Katzenbach admittance to Foster Auditorium (above). A federal judge had ordered the admission of two black students to the University. To Dad it had been a question of state vs. federal control of local institutions.

In 1964 my father ran for President of the United States and a lady who voted for him in one of the primaries sent me this clipping (below). Here we are (right) at the airport in Montgomery when Dad returned from one of these primaries. From left: me, Peggy Sue, Mom, Lee, Dad. My mother's mom, Mrs. Estelle Burns, is behind Peggy.

MEET THE MOST DIE-HARD WALLACE ROOTER IN ALABAMA
It's not that this youngster is prejudiced or any-thing, but carrying a welcome home sign for Gov. George C. Wallace in Montgomery, Ala., is his son, George Jr. The sign proudly proclaims Wallace as the "Greatest American Since Robert E. Lee." A huge crowd cheered the governor.

At first Mother was skeptical when Dad suggested that she
run for Governor in 1966. But she thought it over for a
few months. Then she underwent her first cancer surgery,
believed it to be a success, and grew more optimistic about
life and the idea that she might indeed run successfully
for public office. Mother and Dad traveled the state
making speeches everywhere to large and enthusiastic
crowds. Mother won the primary and easily won
election in November. Here she is (above, right) with
Dad in the inaugural parade on January 16, 1967. "I am
proud to be an Alabamian," she said in her address.

During Mother's years as Governor, Dad remained active in politics. Mother had pledged to carry out the plans and maintain the priorities and policies that he had established as Governor. Here is a photo of Dad with comedian Brother Dave Gardner, a longtime friend. And here he is testifying before Sen. Russell Long's Finance and Taxation Committee in Washington early in 1967. The man behind Dad (above, left) is Billy Watson, Dad's close personal friend and political teacher, who grew up in Clayton and knew several Alabama Governors. He passed away shortly after this picture was taken.

In June, 1967, my mother began to suffer from stomach cramps, and immediately she feared that her cancer had returned. Later that month a biopsy confirmed that another malignancy existed. Here she is (right) with Dad at a baseball game at Dome Stadium, July 6. She was in Houston for cancer surgery. In the fall, she returned to Houston for cobalt treatments, and here she is with Dad and the press on September 9 (right). In November she was strong enough to join Dad in California where he was signing up voters for the American Independent Party in order to get it on the ballot there during his planned 1968 campaign for president. After the first of the year, Mother's condition worsened, though somehow she managed to make an appearance at Wallace-for-President headquarters on January 11. But as spring approached, she became weaker and weaker. She died on May 7, 1968.

After Mother's death, it was months before
Dad could pull himself together. But he knew
that he couldn't stay idle, so he threw himself
into the 1968 presidential campaign. When he
announced his intentions to run in February
(right) he committed himself to the goals of
the average American, and he was still committed. In August he accepted the official
nomination of the American Independent
Party and pledged himself to "Stand Up For
America." I traveled with him everywhere
during that campaign, but I only played at a
couple of his rallies that year. Mostly I was
along to keep him company because he was
still depressed about Mother's death, as was I.
The 1968 Presidential campaign was
rigorous, and though I was amazed at Dad's
popularity outside Alabama, I was shocked to
find some of the crowds pretty hostile. In
some places the crowds were warm and
enthusiastic, like Chicago in September
(opposite). In other places people heckled
him or tried to stop him from finishing his
speeches. I was bothered by this, but Dad
understood that people didn't always understand or agree with him—and that politics is
an area where people feel very deeply. I was
proud of him, but I was worried about his
safety. The crowds were large and after
Dr. Martin Luther King, Jr. and Bobby
Kennedy were killed, I became more and
more concerned about his safety.

§ 154 §

Dad's 1970 race for Governor of Alabama
was a tough one, but he worked harder than
ever. Here he is on the campaign trail at
Collinsville, Alabama, in June 1970 (below).
I traveled across the state with him, singing
and playing my guitar at his rallies. Although
he came in second in the first primary and
forced a runoff with incumbent Governor
Albert Brewer, he ended up winning by 35,000
votes and went on to win the election in
November. This picture (right) was taken at
the 1970 inaugural ball.

UPI

UPI

In 1972 Dad announced to a standing-room-only crowd in the chambers of the Florida senate in Tallahassee that he would be a candidate for the presidency (below, left). I felt good about performing in the 1972 campaign. Dad would be a hard act to follow, but he was also a hard act to precede. I tried to keep the music as excited and up-tempo as the crowds who were waiting to see him. Cornelia, who married Dad in 1971, traveled with him and sat on the platform when he spoke. There was enthusiasm wherever he went, and once in awhile, as in 1968, there was some hostility. My main concern at the rallies was always for him, especially when he was going through a crowd. It was out of one of these large, enthusiastic crowds, at the Laurel shopping center in Maryland, that Arthur Bremer emerged to shoot my father, on May 15, 1972, the day before the Maryland primary.

WTOP-TV Eyewitness News via UPI

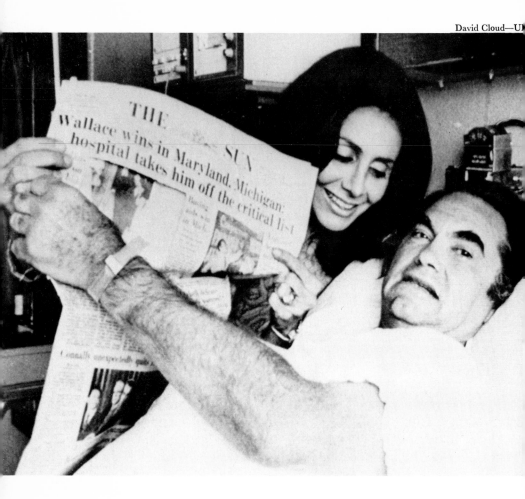

From the moment I learned that my Dad had
not sustained a head wound, I never doubted
that he would live. The day after the
Michigan and Maryland primaries (which he
won) Dad was taken off the hospital's critical
list. And although he knew that his chances
of walking again were "less than 50-50," he
never lost hope. Here he is with Cornelia, who
had so bravely faced the TV cameras to share
her knowledge and her faith that Dad would
be all right.

For more than a year my father was never without pain, yet he never complained. Six weeks after the shooting, the Democratic National Convention was held in Miami, and Dad was there to address the delegates (below). He worked very hard that year, and the next, at being Governor of Alabama, and at learning to stand and walk again. On May 1, 1973, nearly a year after the attempted assassination, he stood for the first time in public to address a joint session of the Alabama legislature. Although paralyzed from the waist down, he stood erect behind a specially-built podium (right).

Through all his troubles Dad still had time to spend with Cornelia, with my sisters and with me. In 1973 I signed with Buddy Lee Attractions, a booking agency in Nashville (below, right), and in August I signed with MGM records.

In 1970 our family posed for this picture at the house on Farrar Street in Montgomery that my mother had wanted so much and had worked for so hard. In the back row, from the left are Peggy Sue, me, Dad, and Jim Parsons, Bobbi's husband. In the second row are Cornelia's son, Jim, Cornelia, Bobbi Jo and little Jimbo, and on the floor are Cornelia's other son, Josh, and my little sister, Lee.

me something in return. But in the end I realized the fraternity wasn't doing very much for me, through no fault of its own, nor was I doing that much for the fraternity. I wasn't going to the parties they had, and all I'd do was eat over there.

And I think music was the reason. I was really thinking about music at that point, and I couldn't get interested in *anything* at the university, really. So when it came time to pledge during the second semester of my freshman year, I decided against it.

It wasn't only my interest in music that kept me from doing so. Once again, although the fellows were very nice, I ran into that old bugaboo of social consciousness that had bothered me in high school.

For instance, if you brought up a girl's name, someone would ask, "What club is she in?" They identified people by clubs, and I could never do that. If a girl was in one sorority she was considered a certain type of person, and if she was in another she was considered another type. But it's not that way with people, and I resented that a little. But you can't fight the fraternity system.

And I think a lot of the guys in the fraternities were striving to have what I already had, so to speak. I was recognized pretty easily on campus. And they were striving for recognition, with their pins and their jerseys and so on. I never cared about that. So I think there was just a difference in interests.

I did pretty well in class, but there were times when I didn't apply myself that much, really, because I'd spend my evenings playing the guitar instead of studying.

So my music interfered with my studies as it had with my fraternity life. It came to be a real conflict between my music and being in school.

I think if I had been interested in what I was studying at school, it would have been different. And I still believe the business courses helped me, because it's good to know about economics and subjects like that whether you become a businessman or not.

But I wasn't ever really into my business courses, even though I had wanted to go to college. Because I had music on my mind.

So during my nearly two years at the University of Alabama I really began to consider for the first time what I wanted to do with my life. And although I made good grades, I found I wasn't interested in the university or a business career.

I realized that music was what I wanted to pursue, and I knew I wouldn't be happy until I did.

I think at one period Dad thought I would follow in his footsteps: the university and law school and maybe eventually politics. So it took him a while to understand my musical ambitions—and to understand the modern music I played, too, because he never was very musical despite having played the guitar a bit.

But now he has come to understand my music and my devotion to it. And that's why, as he has said, he is pulling for me one hundred percent.

Chapter Eleven

•

ON JANUARY 4, 1971, my father at the age of fifty-one married thirty-one-year-old Cornelia Ellis Snively, an olive-skinned beauty with long, flowing black hair. Cornelia was a divorcee with two sons—Jim, who was then eight years old, and seven-year-old Josh. Her mother, the very tall and extremely lively Mrs. Ruby Austin, was famous for the parties she gave as the sister of Gov. James ("Kissin' Jim") Folsom at the old Governor's Mansion when she was his official hostess prior to his second marriage. Miss Ruby is a living legend in Alabama and deserves to be. She even ran for Secretary of State once but didn't make it.

Cornelia was born January 28, 1939, in the front bedroom of her grandmother's home in Elba, Alabama— the town Mother had so much trouble finding once. She's a small-town girl with a sophisticated sheen, but she says, "I still prefer a homey-looking white frame house—yes, one with a swing on the porch." As a matter of fact, she lived in a log cabin for a time during her childhood, an invaluable asset for anyone connected with politics.

"My Grandfather Folsom was a country politician just like George's father and grandfather," she noted recently. And her own involvement with politics goes back a long time.

"Cornelia grew up in politics," Miss Ruby told me. "Lawd, when she was six years old she was foldin' literature for her uncle."

When Big Jim, a widower, won the election, Ruby and Cornelia and Cornelia's father, Charles G. Ellis, and her brother, Charles Junior, moved into the Governor's Mansion with him and his two older daughters.

Cornelia also campaigned for my father a number of times, having known him since her childhood as a supporter of her Uncle Jim's, for whom, as she recalled, he had worked "tooth and toenail."

She wrote a campaign song which my father used in 1958. When she was recently asked to sing it, she began, "Wallace in the morning, Wallace in the evening, Wallace at suppertime," then confessed, "I can't remember the rest."

Cornelia has always been musically inclined, an interest we share, and when she lived at the old Governor's Mansion as a child she once dressed up like a cowgirl and entertained legislators by singing *I'm an Old Cowhand from the Rio Grande* at one of Big Jim's parties.

She also had tea at the White House in 1950, when the piano-playing Harry S Truman was President. In fact, Cornelia once teased my father that if he hadn't skipped out on the piano lessons his mother tried to get him to take, he might already be in the White House. She herself was playing the piano as well as the organ in Montgomery churches at the age of fifteen. Like my sister Lee, who is a national champion, she was also a baton twirler around that time.

While living in the Mansion, Cornelia even served as a page in the legislature, just as my father did. But unlike him she had no desire to be Governor.

Another memory of her childhood in the Mansion is a visit by Hank Williams' widow, Audrey, who brought along Hank Junior, then eight years old. A couple of years ago I toured with Hank Junior's show.

To continue the parallels with the Wallace family, she graduated from my own alma mater, Sidney Lanier High School in Montgomery. While in high school, she played the saxophone. And she competed in the Miss Alabama beauty contest and was chosen a runner-up.

She attended Huntingdon College in Montgomery, as I am doing at present, but later transferred to Rollins College in Orlando, Florida, to study music, voice and piano. She wanted to be a concert pianist, but wound up in country music.

At the age of nineteen, Cornelia learned to play the guitar and started singing professionally—because she wanted to be able to support herself with her music. That year she composed two country-western songs and recorded them for MGM, the record company to which I am under contract. The titles: *Baby with the Barefoot Feet* and *It's No Summer Love.*

Cornelia's mother, Miss Ruby, had accompanied her when she went to Nashville to record. Cornelia remembers sitting on the steps outside the studio when Roger Miller asked her to do a demonstration record of his song, *How Do You Tell It to a Child.* Not long afterward he had a hit record with *In the Summertime,* a forerunner of his *King of the Road*. She also met Minnie Pearl on that trip. Minnie introduced her to columnist Earl Wilson, who wrote about her in his column.

But perhaps the highlight of her musical career was a 1959 tour of the western United States, Hawaii and Australia with a troupe headed by country star Roy Acuff. Cornelia played guitar and sang. She did duets with Melba Montgomery, who later sang for my father's 1972 campaign. In Australia, the troupe filmed TV shows with Roy—the first TV films ever made there.

Returning to her study of serious music, Cornelia went to New York City for a year to study voice under Carlo Menotti and dramatic arts at the Neighborhood Playhouse. She also tried to break into New York show business but without success.

She has admitted, "When I went to New York, they didn't know what to do with me. I wasn't really pure folk, not pure country, not popular music and not rock 'n' roll." She knew what it was to struggle and be short of money in those days.

Then her father, who had been a civil engineer, became seriously ill with cancer, and Cornelia returned home to Montgomery.

In the summer she taught water skiing to Girl Scouts at Camp Kiwanis, having induced the city to buy a boat for that purpose. But worry about her father's health filled her thoughts.

For the last three months of Charles Ellis's life, Cornelia slept every night on a cot in his room at a Montgomery hospital. "It made him feel better for me to be there," she said later. I am reminded of the nights I spent in my mother's hospital suite when she, like Cornelia's father, was dying of cancer.

In Cornelia's case, several years later her stepfather, Dr. Burton Austin, also died of cancer.

Cornelia says she feels a special understanding of what the Wallaces went through during our mother's illness and death because of her own experiences with cancer, which left a lasting mark on her. She was twenty-one when her father died, and for a year she was deeply depressed over his death.

Her recovery from her deep sorrow was aided by an invitation to become a professional water skier at Cypress Gardens in Florida. Her work there kept her too active to brood, and the change in surroundings also helped.

She obtained the job when Dick Pope, manager of Cypress Gardens, was visiting a relative who lived next door to the Ellises and invited her to work at the Gardens. She was there for a year and a half as a skier and also as a model.

At one time she was the star of the ski show as the swan ballerina, executing the difficult "Backward Swan" number. But later she attempted to ski barefoot and injured her chest, and was told not to ski anymore. So she concentrated on other aquatic feats and modeling from then on. A talented horsewoman, she also captured the grand prize at Florida horse shows with her entry, "Mr. Cypress Gardens."

She met her first husband, John Snively, III, of Winter Haven, Florida, while she was working at Cypress Gardens. They were married seven years, and although the marriage produced two sons she was active in civic groups in Florida, including the Polk County League of Women Voters. She also aided cancer drives in the area, knowing from first-hand observation the ravages of the disease and the heartbreak it brings to entire families.

After her first marriage ended, Cornelia returned to Montgomery with Jim and Josh and lived with her mother. Early in 1970 she renewed acquaintances with my father, who was then preparing to run for Governor.

"Cornelia used to spend a lot of time next door with my neighbors, Tom and Sue Johnson," her mother told me in explaining how the courtship began. "Tom is editor of the *Montgomery Independent*. Their children were over here all the time with Jim and Josh. They're the same age, so the boys became real good friends.

"And George would drop by next door to visit Tom, because they're very close. So when Cornelia and George were both visiting the Johnsons, they just started talking to each other. It was not a courtship for a long time."

"George felt comfortable with me," Cornelia has said, pointing out, "We've always known each other. In politics you develop this kind of mistrust about people you don't know. You ask, 'Are they using you?' "

"So it just started from there, and soon they were talking to each other on the phone," Miss Ruby recalls. "They were seeing each other before and all during the campaign."

Dad visited Miss Ruby's house to see Cornelia, and sometimes we children visited the house, too. "But we didn't go out much," Cornelia admits. "Frankly, neither of us wanted to be exposed to all the publicity."

And, in fact, a lot of people with fond memories of my mother didn't think Dad should remarry. "And they told him so," Cornelia admits.

So their courtship was largely confined to phone calls, dinners at Miss Ruby's house or our house on Farrar, and dining at a few out-of-the-way restaurants.

"I thought it was silly," Cornelia has said in that frank way of hers. "But publicity would have been embarrassing if the romance had had a big split."

By the time of the wedding, two weeks before Dad's inauguration, all of us had gotten to know Cornelia well, and she and I had played the guitar together at Miss Ruby's house. During the summer of 1970, Cornelia had taken Lee water skiing at Lee's request.

"What do you think first drew Dad and Cornelia together?" I asked Miss Ruby recently, as we were having a long conversation in the Mansion about her daughter.

"Politics, I guess!" she quickly replied. "After all, Cornelia grew up in politics when we lived with James and were goin' to all his speakin's."

She told me about the first time Cornelia had ever met my father and mother—when Cornelia was only seven years old.

"When James was Governor and we had parties at the old Mansion, your parents always came to the parties. George was in the legislature. And I'd generally let the children visit around and meet the guests. I wanted to teach them to be hospitable and learn the correct things to do when they got older, like my mama taught *me*. And all the guests were crazy about them, because they were nicely behaved. Cornelia and Rachel were about seven, Melissa was about four, and Charles was about nine.

"One evening during a party the girls were sitting on the stairs. I had sent them up with the maid to get undressed and ready for bed, and they weren't supposed to come back down. Because I was visitin' around, and we were having a dance and dinner party. We had a beautiful place to dance in that old Mansion.

"And they had put their gowns on—an Italian girl had made them, and they looked like evening dresses, they were so pretty. And they sat on the stairs. It was a beautiful staircase, and each of them was looking through the banister at the people dancing.

"Lurleen saw them, and she went up and hugged and kissed them. George will remember that, because he was with her. Lurleen said they were all so cute, looking through the banister at everybody.

"You know, it was Cornelia who picked out the Governor's Mansion you're living in now," Miss Ruby pointed out. "One day when Cornelia was eight years old she went for a walk with James, while we were all living in the old Governor's Mansion. It's since been torn down.

"James loved to walk in the afternoon, when it was possible. And we hadn't been living in the old Mansion too long before they walked down *this* way.

"Cornelia saw this house and she said, '*This* is a *beautiful* mansion. This is so much prettier than that old, ugly Mansion *we* live in. I wish *this* was the Mansion.'

"And he said, 'You do, Cornelia?' And she said, 'Yes, Sir.'

"So he said, 'We'll just stop and knock on the door and see who lives here, and see if we can buy it!'

"So he did. And when Buster, the butler, came to the door, he said, 'Oh, my God, my Lord, Mister Big Jim! It's the Governor! Lord, how you doin'?'

"James said, 'Fine, fine. What's your name?'

"And he said, 'I'm Buster, Miz Ligon's butler.'

"James said, 'Well, is the lady of the house here?'

"And Buster said, 'No, she's gone to Washington to see Miss Emily, and she's not here.'

"James said, 'Well, my little niece here, Cornelia, thinks this is a pretty house, and she wants that we ought to buy this for the Governor's Mansion.' And he said, 'I think it's a good idea *myself*.'

"So Buster said, 'You want to see the house, Governor?'

"James said, 'Yes.' So Buster carried them through the house. And they had a little train back there, a chair that carried Miz Ligon up and down the back stairs.

"Buster said, 'When Miz Ligon comes home I'll tell her you all want to buy the mansion. Of course, I don't think she would *sell* it, but I'll *tell* her.'

"When she got back from Washington, she called the wife of one of the Supreme Court justices, who was a good friend of ours and hers also, and asked her if she could give a party here for us.

"And she did. Miz Ligon had a seated dinner for about—how many will this place seat?—I 'spect about 300 people, pretty near.

"So she told James, she said, 'Governor Folsom, I heard that you wanted to buy my house for the Mansion.'

"He said, 'Yeah—sure do.'

"She said, 'Well, if anything happens to me before you go out of office, I have already told Emily.' Her daughter, Emily, had married into the Mellon family. 'She would never live in it. And Emily being an only child, I would *love* for it to go to the Governor's Mansion.' So that's what she told him that night she had this party for us.

"And we became very good friends, and after that we had her at the Mansion and so forth.

"So she died six months before James went out of

office, and he bought the Mansion, and paid $100,000, I believe. Governor Persons was Governor-elect, so they remodeled it and he moved into it."

"And now Cornelia is First Lady here," I observed.

"Yes—living in the Mansion she picked out!" Miss Ruby exclaimed.

She leaned closer. "There's been a slightly different story told about it, but it wasn't that way—that she needed to go to the little girls' room, and that's why they stopped. But that's not the way it was!" she laughed. "The way I told it's the way it was."

"What was Dad like when he was in the legislature?" I asked Miss Ruby.

"Well, he was real smart—had a good head on him! He was James's right-hand man; James named Wallace Trade School after him. James stood in with Truman and we got everything; he got rural electrification and all kinds of things for Alabama. Even later, when George and James were rivals politically, I don't guess there was ever any bad feeling between them.

"When George and I get together, I like to talk politics and he does, too," Miss Ruby observed. "I want to interrupt and Cornelia wants me to keep my mouth shut.

"I liked Lurleen, too," Miss Ruby added. "When she ran for Governor, I thought, 'Well, that's just the most impossible thing in the world. *No* woman can be elected Governor of Alabama! George must have lost his cotton-pickin' mind.' But she turned out to have a lot of spunk.

"Her speech at the inauguration was just unbelievable. She gave it so beautiful you'd have thought she'd been studying speech and had finished college and had taught it, she did such a good job. She sounded like a seasoned politician who had been speaking all her life."

"Did you used to talk to Mother much?"

"Yes, I'd see her in the beauty parlor and we'd talk politics. She was always pleasant. We went to Berniece Moeller's beauty college, where it was cheap. We didn't have to pay but a dollar. This was both before and after she was elected.

"I would compliment her on the things she was doing, and she'd ask about Cornelia. Just women's talk. Nothing *deep* politically."

Lee is the apple of her eye. "Lee is just crazy about Jim and Josh," she notes happily. "They can all swim like fish! She's called Cornelia 'Mother' from the very beginning, and she called me 'Grandma' even before the wedding!

"Lee and the boys used to play with each other and enjoy each other so much—she was tomboyish. She isn't now. I guess age and Cornelia getting her into other interests have gotten her out of that. Cornelia's just as attentive, or even more so, to Lee as she is to the boys.

"She sees to it that she has everything that a little girl should have—piano lessons, organ lessons—and since Lee's interested in baton, Cornelia promotes that. And she gets beautiful clothes for her."

Ruby is proud of her daughter's achievements as Alabama's First Lady and her constant interest in improving the Governor's Mansion. And in this regard she told me one more story about her daughter.

"You know, Cornelia has often sung for the prisoners who work at the Mansion. And they just love it.

"Well, the night she and George had the legislature

over for dinner, there was just one woman legislator there. She asked me did I think Cornelia would sing, and I told her I just didn't know, although she *had* been singing for the *prisoners*. I said, '*You'd* better ask her!'

"So she did. And Ferlin Husky was there. And Cornelia said no *way* was she going to sing for the legislators with Ferlin Husky—although she had already sung with him for the prisoners. The mikes and amplifiers weren't exactly right that evening.

"But finally she sang by herself, and did real well. It really went over with the legislature.

"But before she started, she said, 'Well, I said I'd sing a song for you. But you've heard people sing for their supper? Well, I'm singing for the *paint* on the Mansion.' Seems she wanted the Mansion redecorated. And it went over so big, the next day or two they appropriated enough money to redecorate the house and buy some extra land around it as well."

Miss Ruby concluded our conversation by saying, "All the people that love my brother love George. And people were really torn between whom to support when they ran against each other. Because the same people that voted for George were the people that loved James so much.

"After George and Cornelia were married, everybody was so pleased about it. And I said, 'Well, I'll tell you. George defeated James, and I just said, "Heck with it! If you can't beat 'em, join 'em." And I just married my daughter off to him. Because I believe in keeping the Governorship in the family.'

"Cornelia said, 'Mother, I hear that everywhere I go. And you *know* you didn't have anything to do with that!'

"And I said, 'Well, I had a *little* bit. I mean, you *are* my *daughter....*'"

And Miss Ruby laughed contentedly. Then she sighed, "It was a *beautiful* wedding, down here at Trinity Church. And I had a seated dinner for her family and George's family."

Cornelia's first public appearance as Mrs. George Wallace came on Inauguration Eve, 1971, at the first inaugural concert in Alabama history. It featured young performing artists of Alabama, including Cornelia's cousin, Linda Folsom Ottsen, an opera singer who is a former Miss Alabama.

And on January 18, 1971, she stood with Dad as he took the oath as Governor of Alabama on the Capitol steps.

That afternoon she made her social debut as First Lady at the Governor's Mansion when she and Dad hosted a reception where many Barbour countians were present. It was the start of a busy schedule for Cornelia which has never let up.

Within the next few months, among other engagements she had appeared at a Chamber of Commerce dinner in Greenville, at a Fraternal Order of Police convention and a concert in Birmingham, a March of Dimes telorama in Montgomery, and had hosted a tea for Heart Fund workers and a coffee get-together for Cancer Crusade workers at the Mansion.

She even drove the pace car for the Winston 500 race at Alabama International Speedway, practicing for the event at speeds that exceeded 110 miles per hour. She later admitted, "During the practice run I was a little nervous." But she took part in the event not only because she is proud of our state's motor speedway, but in order to call attention to Mental Health Month.

As she said, "It was a tremendous thrill for me, and an honor to lead these skilled drivers out to race. I particularly hoped that all who watched this exciting sporting event would give some thought to a cause I am most vitally interested in—that of our mentally retarded children."

On another occasion, true to Dad's teetotaling ways, she used a bottle of Clayton spring water instead of champagne to christen the seventh and final steel core of the Interstate Highway 10 tunnel at a launching ceremony in Mobile. It was a part of Dad's interstate highway program. Lee was there with her to see the tunnel section go splashing into the water.

Later that day Cornelia managed to put in a plug for her program to obtain authentic historical objects for the Governor's Mansion, including belongings of each of Alabama's former Governors. Among items she had already been promised were a chandelier and a carpet for the main entrance hall. The carpet, which is now in place, bears Alabama's state coat of arms.

Her busy schedule as First Lady hasn't tired her. "I love being active and I thrive on being involved," she once explained.

But she still finds plenty of time for her family—a family which was considerably expanded when she became a stepmother of four upon marrying Dad.

And that's not all.

"I married and became a grandmother all in the same day and I love it," Cornelia said recently. For my sister, Bobbi Jo, often drops by the Mansion on weekends with her husband and their small sons.

Cornelia loves to give family parties. She hadn't been

in the Mansion for a week when she hosted a dinner for Peggy and her friends to celebrate Peggy's twenty-first birthday.

Not long afterward she gave a roller-skating party for her sons, Jim and Josh. And she put on a pair of skates herself and joined the children in their skating.

She once held a "western party" for the kids, complete with a make-believe hold-up staged by older children she had persuaded to dress up as villains—with other children dressed as "good guys" to oppose them.

Remembering that her first duty is as a wife, however, Cornelia schedules her appointments around Dad's so they can be together as much as possible. He comes home for lunch daily from the Capitol, and weekends are spent at the Mansion with the children.

On a Sunday morning you're likely to find Dad sunning in the backyard in his wheelchair with his shirt off, and Cornelia lying next to him on a chaise longue in her bathing suit, as they go through the Sunday papers.

But they're churchgoers, too, dividing their attendance between Dad's church, St. James Methodist, and Cornelia's church, Trinity Presbyterian.

One Sunday afternoon Cornelia was upstairs looking for Dad when one of the children said, "Mother, he's downstairs making a speech to all those people. It's something about the house and it's important, because he's been talking a long time."

It turned out that Dad had learned some people from a hardware convention were taking a tour of the Mansion, and he had decided to show them around himself.

What with her official duties and her family responsibilities, Cornelia notes, "I haven't had too much time for my music. But since I've been in the Mansion I've written a few songs and play guitar and piano a little."

Dad's mother, Mozelle, approves completely of Cornelia. There's no mother-in-law trouble between them.

She says Cornelia is the most wonderful thing that could have happened to Dad since Mother's death. "He was the loneliest person after Lurleen died," she realizes. "Children are wonderful, but they couldn't fill the gap left by their mother."

I was personally very touched by something Cornelia told writer Anita Smith, who wrote a wonderful book several years ago about Mother's life and her courageous struggle with cancer.

"People have been so nice to me since I married George, and I do appreciate it so, so much," Cornelia said. "You know, people could have resented me, because they loved Lurleen so much. . . . And I can see why they did love her."

And she told Anita that she still recalled the words Mother spoke to her when Cornelia was a little girl on the stairway of the old Governor's Mansion, on that memorable evening when Mother and Dad went up the stairs to speak to Cornelia and her cousins: "Now, please don't run back upstairs just now. We all want to see you. You're so pretty."

Although Cornelia is a distinctly different personality from my mother, she shares the interest Mother had in improving the state's facilities for the mentally ill and mentally retarded.

Like Mother, she was visibly shaken following a tour with Dad of Partlow State School and Bryce Hospital. And she vowed to use her energies and influence to relieve their most critical needs, building on the pioneer work done by my mother in those respects. Times change, and such facilities always need updating.

She also is interested in the rehabilitation of the state's prisoners.

Lest anyone forget that such goals have not only human value but are an actual saving to taxpayers, she recently noted that "Mental patients and prisoners are liabilities to taxpayers. They should be rehabilitated or trained and restored to society so that they can at least support themselves."

Cornelia not only loves my father—she defends him strongly against his critics. I would like to quote some words she spoke on the NBC News "Comment" show:

"The press, as a rule, has disagreed with the stand my husband has taken on certain political issues. Journalists have referred to him as a racist and a bigot.

"I believe George Wallace has been misunderstood because his motives have been misinterpreted. . . .

"He is a man who is motivated by a need to help other people. He never has been and never could be a man motivated by personal or financial gain. As a child, he was known for small acts of kindness, such as bringing a friend home to lunch because the friend had no money. The programs he has supported since he served in public office show his sincerity for the needs of the people. . . .

"It has often been said of George, if his enemies could spend an hour with him, they would change their opinion of him and I have seen this happen many times.

"The children and I wish everyone could know him as the kind, considerate, affectionate man we know at home."

She has also said of Dad, "He's very accomplished—as a man, a politician and a public servant.

"Some of his political views have not been very popular but he was representing what the people of Alabama wanted and he represented them well."

She declared that all the programs he has introduced and supported have been "to help the underprivileged people of all races and creeds. We have no racial discrimination."

But she frankly admitted that she was speaking of official policies and programs, not in terms of social discrimination by private citizens.

"There is no universal attitude," she said of such private actions, which are outside the scope of government. "Everybody has his own attitude."

Cornelia is particularly amusing when she tells about the time she and Dad visited the White House during a midwinter Governors' conference held in Washington. "The highlight of the conference took place on the first night we were in Washington," she remembers. "It was a seated dinner at the White House in honor of the Governors and their wives, hosted by President and Mrs. Nixon.

"We dressed in our most formal attire and went down to await our car." Since, as I have noted, it's my father's policy to use an inexpensive automobile, he had rented a white sedan to use in Washington.

When the car arrived, Cornelia continues, "We got in and headed toward 1600 Pennsylvania Avenue. As we approached the gate, I noticed a long line of black limousines. It suddenly occurred to me that perhaps we should have rented a larger car, or at least a black one! I wondered if they would permit us to enter the gate.

"I was a little apprehensive as one of the White

House guards lowered his head, guest list in hand, and peered into the back window of our car. He jerked back to attention, gave a flashy salute and said, 'Yes, Sir, Governor Wallace, go right in, Sir!' "

Inside the White House, an aide informed Dad and Cornelia that protocol with Governors is the order in which their state was admitted to the Union.

And Cornelia admits, "I mischievously inquired, 'Which time?' Our aide's serious exterior melted into a grin as he answered, 'The last time doesn't count.' "

After dinner and a performance by Bob Hope, President and Mrs. Nixon invited everyone to dance and excused themselves and retired to their private quarters.

Suddenly Cornelia noticed several unattended females. "As I watched in curiosity, they came through the crowd straight at my husband!"

They were, Cornelia discovered, the Women's Press Corps. And she adds with a laugh, "And there I witnessed it: George C. Wallace holding his first press conference at the White House unannounced, unintentional, and unknown to the resident President."

Was it a portent of things to come? Only the future will tell.

Recently Cornelia and I sat in the beautiful bedroom she shares with Dad and talked about her views on her life and our family, now that she has been Mrs. George Wallace for several years.

How does she feel about being the stepmother of four, as well as the mother of two children of her own—and how does she cope with the task? As one of those four stepchildren, I was particularly interested in her answers, which she gave with her usual frankness.

"Lee's so close to the ages of *my* children, just a couple of years older, that I just treat her like I treat my own two boys," she observed.

Then she frowned as she confessed, "It bothers me a good bit to be away from them, because I feel like young children need their parents with them as much as possible.

"And of course we're away a lot. That's the only thing that really frustrates me about having a husband in the political limelight. Because, as you know, I travel with George and I did all during his campaigns.

"But if I traveled with him, I always felt a little frustrated because I didn't have the children with me. And if I stayed home with the children, then I felt frustrated because I didn't have my husband.

"It's very hard to get the family all together. So that's why, when we were campaigning in 1972, we always came in on Saturday nights and could at least spend Sunday here with the family. We never stayed away two weeks at a time.

"And then, on trips that we thought would be educational or otherwise beneficial to them, if they wouldn't have to miss school, we would have them come where we were. And of course they loved traveling and had a great time.

"With you *older* children, that was a big adjustment for *me*," she confessed. "Because, as you know, I had not been able to go with you through your younger years, had not been able to shape you in any way, to shape your character or your habits or anything.

"In fact, you were the last one of George's children that I met," she recalled. "I had seen Bobbi and Peggy

Sue and Lee before I met you at dinner one night at the house on Farrar. I didn't really know you until then.

"Let's see—Peggy turned 21 the first year we were here, you turned 20, and Bobbi Jo was about 27 and married. So what could I do? I couldn't come in with children of your age and start telling you how to run your lives because your personalities and habits were already established.

"So what I tried to do with you and Peggy Sue from the first was just keep an open door for you to come to me with your problems, and try to show a little interest in what you were doing . . . ask you about your friends, or if you wanted to take trips with us a few times a year.

"Mostly you and Peggy were in and out, and seeing you at mealtime was the highlight of our being with you.

"I know how my brother used to be," Cornelia smiled. "He didn't like to talk about his personal life around his mother or daddy or around me. So we never asked him about his dates or anything too much.

"And I kind of feel you're the same way, you know," Cornelia told me. "If you mention it, then I ask you about it. But I don't feel that I should question you about your dates every time you come in. I think you would resent that.

"I just try to be available to listen to you and talk to you, but I really try not to pry into your personal affairs.

"As for Peggy Sue, she's a girl and I think I was able to help her through two or three emotional adjustments as she was growing up. I put a little more time into her, because she would come to me for advice. So I had some pretty good sessions with her.

"It's hard, when you have six children, to get to spend a little time with one of them when the others aren't around," Cornelia observed. "But I've enjoyed the times you and I have played the guitar together in your room and have sung duets. I'm sorry we don't get to do it more often, but you've been in school most of the time, or on a date, or our schedules have conflicted.

"I'll never forget the time you and your dad and I did 'The Mike Douglas Show' right after he and I were married," she smiled. "They really wanted the Governor on, and they asked me because nobody had seen me much, and they wanted you to sing.

"When the three of us went up to Philadelphia, George was very nervous. And you and I were really *not* nervous. You were singing and playing your song, kind of warming up for the show. And you know I always cut a fool a little bit. I was tap dancing around and shuffling my feet and clapping my hands, remember?

"And your daddy sat there, and he started just getting *so nervous*. I think any time that he goes on television, if he's got to do something with his family, he never knows what they're going to say, and that's what makes him afraid.

"He'll go out there and say everything just right, just the way it ought to be, and not say anything that would hurt him politically. But when we were backstage at 'The Mike Douglas Show,' he couldn't be responsible for a son and a new wife! And the longer we waited to go on, the more nervous he got.

"He looked at me and said, 'What are you going to say? What are you going to say?'

"I said, 'Well, George, I don't know what they're going to *ask* me yet.'

"He said, 'Get the questions. Get the questions brought to you.' So they brought the list of questions.

"And he said, 'All right, how are you going to answer that question?'

"I said, 'Well, George, it's no big deal. I'm just going to give a straight answer, because I'm honest.'

"He said, 'All right. Well, let's see. . . . How are you going to answer *that* question?'

"You know, if somebody's nervous like that, it tends to become contagious. You were beginning to get fidgety, and it was even beginning to make *me* nervous.

"And I said, 'Well, look. If this is making you all this nervous about what I'm going to say, I won't say *anything*. I'll just go up there and sing with George Junior and solve *that* problem.'

"So you and I agreed that we would sing together, remember?" she smiled. "I wondered, 'Well, what can I think of where we could sing harmony and sound nice?'

"So I was trying to teach you *You Are My Sunshine*. We were just going to go out and sing it as a duet and be done with it. So we rehearsed it a little bit.

"And then, about the time we got the thing rehearsed a little—and really, I think we could have done it very well—they came and took you away, let *you* perform, and then it ended up with them coming back and getting your daddy and me and taking us on the show to talk.

"So we didn't get to do our duet, did we?" she laughed. "But it was a lot of fun. It was kind of a nice experience, a time that we got to be together, just the three of us.

"Of course, I'm glad that you bring your new tapes to us right away when you make a recording. And I naturally identify with you a lot, because from the time I married your father you've been going through the same thing *I* was going through when I made my record—and after I made my record, trying to do the stage shows and find somebody to put it all together for me.

"In my case," she admitted, "I had a good record company. I had a good manager. I had a lot of things— but I just never got it all together for anybody to really *package* me, I guess.

"I've tried very hard not to *over*-encourage you, because I think my natural tendency is to say, 'Yeah, go on—*do* that thing. It's *great*.' But your father wants you to go to school and get an education, so I just try to let you know how interested I am in what you're doing, how talented I think you are.

"But I try real hard not to say, 'Yeah, go on out there. You're going to be a big star.' Because I think if you have it in you, you have to push *yourself,* and get the experience to develop on your own. So I leave that part of it up to you.

"But I always like to listen to your tapes," Cornelia smiled, "and I get thrilled and excited over them, although I promise I'll always try to tell you frankly if I ever think any of them can be improved."

True to her word, Cornelia *has* always been frank with me. And now I'll tell you what I think of Cornelia.

I admire Cornelia. I admire the way she has functioned as First Lady of the state.

Of course, she's a very outspoken woman, as you can see from the television shows she's done and from what she has told me for this book.

She would never be content to stay home and just be First Lady in the Mansion, although she runs the Mansion very well. She likes to get out and do things, as you can tell from all her activities.

How do I feel about my father having remarried? Well, that's what Daddy wanted, so if *he* wanted it, of course *I* want it.

I can't make a comparison between Cornelia and my mother, because you only have one mother, you know. But I think Cornelia has been good for Lee, and I thought she would be at the time she married Dad.

Personally, I was already in college by then, and I didn't *need* any mothering. And she never tried to be a mother to me. She's not that much older than I am, really.

But she's always been very interested in my career, as she has said, and willing to help me any way she *could* help me, in that or anything else.

I've enjoyed the times I've sat and played guitar while she sang here at the Mansion, especially when we did some Hank Williams songs together. She has a strong voice—she likes to belt a song!

Although she has written songs and I have, too, our musical styles are different when it comes to writing. Her music is country and western, while mine is more progressive folk, although I hate labels.

In fact, you can't label Cornelia. She's an original. She's just *herself,* and has made Daddy happy by being that way. And for that I'm very glad—and very grateful to her.

Chapter Twelve

THREE OR FOUR years ago my father and I were sunning on the sand together in Gulf Shores, sitting side by side in beach chairs. It was one of the few times we were ever alone on a beach, and he seemed to be enjoying it as much as I was. We were amused when some people passed us and their faces suddenly registered their shock and surprise at running into George Wallace. They waved at him and he waved back, and we continued our conversation.

On the rare occasions when we're alone together, sometimes I feel like a reporter, because there's so much I want to ask him.

That day I asked if he really wanted to be President. And he told me, "If the people want me I'll be glad to serve. I feel like I'm a spokesman for our movement."

Now, that quote sounds exactly like what he's said countless times in public, right? I know it. My point is just that: the public George Wallace and the private

George Wallace are one and the same when it comes to his views on political affairs. He is telling his true views in both cases, and does not hide his ambitions behind false disclaimers.

However, there *is* something he said to someone else that he did not tell me. For he did not want to alarm me. I heard about it later.

Before he was shot, I asked him about the dangers of running for President, and he tried to keep me from worrying, seeking to minimize the risks.

But early in his 1972 campaign for the Presidency, when he was entering Democratic primaries around the nation, a friend of his was talking to my father in the Governor's office at the Capitol. And he was concerned about my dad's safety.

"George," he predicted gloomily, "you're going to keep on and someone's going to *shoot* you."

And Dad replied, "Well, if it takes that to change the direction of this country, it will *take* that."

But at the beginning of 1972, the year which would so drastically change the life of our family, I had no great forebodings. I was by now a sophomore at the University of Alabama, and concerned with my own life on campus— and what would follow it.

I could still feel the hostility of those students who were against my father and deliberately shunned me, but I was far more concerned with improving as a musician. I practiced alone or sometimes with my friend, Steve Morgan. We both played acoustical guitar, and in my room we'd change around, alternating at playing lead and rhythm. We played rock and some country things.

At that point the frustrations I'd felt about my music when I first went to the university—loving to sing and play guitar but going to class to prepare for quite another career—were tearing me apart at times.

Although I knew now that I wanted to be a musician, I still wasn't quite sure enough of myself to take any decisive action. I didn't want to disappoint my father's hopes that I would someday follow in his footsteps—hopes I suppose I had shared at some point, as something taken for granted. Yet when I was totally honest with myself I realized the political arena was not where I wanted to be.

Finally I ended my inner conflict. I dropped out of school in February, 1972. It was entirely my own decision, because Dad was very definitely against it and tried to talk me out of it.

That was the first time I had ever gone against my father's wishes in a major matter. And even though he accepted my decision without rancor, it was not easy for me. It caused me a lot of private heartache, because I hated to disappoint this man I loved and idolized.

But in a sense I was quitting college to join him. For I knew I was going to be campaigning with him soon, and that cheered me considerably.

And, furthermore, I had signed with a small record company and was trying to get something going along that line.

That experience taught me a lot about the negative side of the music business.

The people who owned the company weren't what they said they were. They didn't have the distribution or the promotion they claimed. They had nothing. I had started writing my own songs, but the one song I wrote for the company during our association, *Plastic Smile*, got nowhere. It was a good record, but it just didn't have the proper resources behind it.

I soon realized that the owners were trying to make it

on my name alone. They didn't care about the quality of the product. They weren't interested in anything but shipping a product with my name on it. It could have been *anything* on the record, as long as it had my name.

They even called me after Daddy got hurt and wanted me to rush and cut something so they could release it. Of course I refused, but I wasn't quite that friendly. I let them know in no uncertain terms that I wasn't going to do it. So I let the contract expire.

From that experience I learned how important exposure is to a recording artist. Of course, some people think my name helps and some think it hurts. As you know, I think it does both.

For instance, take a music director at a radio station who's politically against my dad. That's likely to keep him from playing my record. And if he's *for* my dad, he might play it because of that. But I would be just as insulted in either case. I would like people in the music industry to judge George Wallace, Jr.'s records on quality and disregard the name.

I wasn't always that mature about it. When I was fifteen or sixteen and Mother had won the election, in my youthful naiveté I did a novelty record called *Papa Was Governor Till Mama Moved In*. Believe it or not, it sold quite well. But since then I've come to hope I could make it on my own.

Yet, as I've said, I have done TV talk shows where I've found myself in the position of discussing or even defending my dad and trying to further my career at the same time.

At one point when I had just signed with that small record company, I guested with Dick Cavett, Virginia Graham and David Frost, all within about a week's time, to promote my record for the company, even though the record had no distribution in New York, where the programs originated.

I did my best to handle the situation well, and in fact received a commendation from the State Legislature for the way in which I had represented Alabama. I was relatively new to the music industry, so after performing my song and talking three or four minutes about my career, I would talk with the host or hostess about Dad, and everyone was very interested in his activities and his plans for the future.

I've never minded when such questions arise, and I'm glad to answer them. Because at such times I'm really pulling for Dad as much as for myself, or even more so. In fact, I'm even able to kid about him at times, when that seems appropriate.

On "The Dick Cavett Show" I presented Dick with a George Wallace wrist watch. He asked me if it ever stopped running. I said, "No, it runs continuously to the right."

Not long after leaving college in early 1972, I joined my father's campaign in Florida. I played mostly country music for his audiences, backed by a small group. I did *Jambalaya* and *Ruby* and *Folsom Prison,* a song the audiences particularly loved. And I did *Your Cheatin' Heart* because Dad likes it.

I felt good about performing in the 1972 campaign. I could see my improvements all along—I was getting better at just getting on stage and keeping it together. You can't let outside forces mess up your concentration when you're playing, because your performance has to be nice and smooth.

The audiences seemed to like me, but I knew they were there to see Dad and were eagerly anticipating his appearance. He would be a hard act to follow, and he was a hard act to precede. I usually played up-tempo numbers like *Wildwood Flower*. When people are there to see a man and they're excited, you don't try to put them to sleep.

At these places, country music was what they wanted most. So Dad had a country band and Billy Grammer, a highly popular country performer, traveling with us. Billy is an extremely nice person as well as a fine entertainer with a good stage appearance. At a couple of places they had a local rock band that played because they had young people there and they thought it was appropriate.

After the music, Dad would speak for about an hour. Cornelia sat on the stage while he spoke. There were also a few appearances by Lee and Jim and Josh. But it was such a fast pace, and we had baggage to keep up with—if you're traveling with a Presidential candidate, you've got to be ready. The children were so young it really wasn't practical for them to travel with the campaign much. It could even have been dangerous for them.

Dad won what *Time* magazine called "a stunning 42 percent plurality" in the Florida primary against ten other candidates. And I think his rivals were really surprised when he did so well. Sen. Edmund Muskie, who trailed in fourth place, criticized Dad afterward as a demagogue. And that was politically very naive.

But if my father's big win—"the greatest victory of his turbulent political life" according to *Time*—surprised others, I doubt it surprised *him*. For he could read the pulse of the crowds with unbelievable accuracy.

His slogan in '72 was "Send them a message," and I think that was the beginning, in Florida. The message was being sent all the way till he was taken out of it. It was basically the same message as in 1968—law and order and local control over local institutions.

But busing was a big issue in Florida. The other candidates didn't seem to know what to say about it, and I think they'd get together with their aides and try to figure out how to approach it.

Well, Dad's not that way. He looks at things as they are and he believes what he says, and you can never question his sincerity.

He won votes in Florida because busing was a sensitive issue (and became an important issue elsewhere as well), but he was talking about busing before the Florida primary and none of the other candidates were. He *believed* busing was wrong. He wasn't just trying to win votes. He didn't rely on speech writers. He could talk about the issues without a prepared speech. That's a sure sign of somebody who knows what he believes in.

So he sent them a message—and it all started here in Alabama, even before it took off in Florida. The people of this state started it. He's their spokesman, and it's caught on. People are waking up.

For so many years the South has been looked upon as a backward section of the country, full of racism. But really there's more racism in large urban areas in the northern and western parts of the United States than there has *ever* been in Alabama.

I know we've had some problems. We've had demonstrations. But we've never had a major race riot where people have been killed and looting has taken place.

The Selma-to-Montgomery march was blown so out of proportion. When the initial march began and they were crossing the bridge, they had some violence there. But there are a number of things you have to consider.

I believe from the films of the march that some of the people on it were just there to instigate violence. And you have to remember the policemen standing there try-ing to do *their* job, and the abuse they had to take.

Traveling with Dad, I've seen policemen all over the country having to make a show of strength. And a police-man is only human, and has only so much restraint. He's not a robot. And when he's spit upon, he reacts. But he's there to enforce the law.

I'm not comparing sections of the country, but I'm just showing that when the press has made it appear that it's so dangerous in Alabama, it's been hypocritical. Be-cause it's not really that way.

The races get along well in Alabama—very well. It's not a token thing. I think the South in race relations is far superior to the North today. People don't have hate on their faces down here. In some of the large urban areas in the North, different groups in the community look on each other with hate and contempt. You can't live that way. And we don't have any of that. *I* haven't seen any.

When Dad was speaking out for segregation, I think he felt that as far as the races were concerned you could let things evolve. As I've said, he's not a racist and never *has* been a racist. He's done more for blacks in Alabama than most people realize. And he's never made a speech that reflected on anyone because of race or color and he never will.

When he made the segregation speech that thrust him into the national spotlight at his first inauguration, he was speaking for the way he thought the people of Alabama felt—and they overwhelmingly felt that way. At that point in time, 1963, segregation was quite evident everywhere in the South. But he's human and he has grown and matured, and he's learned a lot of things dur-ing his years in office. So he has changed his views on segregation. And the people of our state have matured and changed, too.

But if you want to pin it down and say, "Well, he said this and now he's changed to this," you can take most other national leaders, and *their* changes in viewpoint are often greater than with my dad. Man shouldn't be constant but should change when change is necessary.

After Florida I spent a good bit of time with Dad campaigning in Michigan and Maryland, and a few days in Indiana. In Michigan it was very cold and snowed a lot, but we had good crowds there as everywhere.

I remember in Kalamazoo, Michigan, there were some hecklers, and I was heckled pretty badly when I got out on stage. They knew who I was, because I'd been introduced, and they were just giving me the same treatment they were going to give Dad. They were shouting and booing.

So when I started to perform, I did one song, and then I went to introduce my guitar player. And they were still booing, so I just stopped talking. They seemed to quiet down a little, because they didn't know I was going to stop talking.

And I said, "You know, when I was growing up my dad gave me a book to read. And the name of that book is *How to Behave in a Crowd*." And at that point the people who were *for* Dad laughed and shouted the hecklers down, and I got a standing ovation. So we did one more song and left the stage. I think I got the best of them, because they weren't expecting me to say what I did. But that was really my first experience with a large crowd of hecklers, and they're hard for me to deal with.

Later, in press photographs of the Kalamazoo crowd, the face of a blond, thin young man was seen clearly. He was twenty-one-year-old Arthur Bremer of Milwaukee,

Wisconsin, and he was my father's would-be assassin. Apparently he had been quietly stalking him around the country. But he had not chosen that day to strike.

At another city in Michigan, we pulled up to the back entrance of an auditorium where Dad was going to speak. Our path was lined with hostile demonstrators for twenty-five to thirty yards between the car and the auditorium, with only a narrow pathway between them.

I preceded my dad, who hadn't arrived yet. But already people were booing and catcalling and waving signs that read WALLACE GO HOME and IF YOU LIKED HITLER YOU'LL LOVE WALLACE. It was one of my first experiences in such a violent atmosphere. I didn't feel physical fear, but I realized the possibilities of what could happen.

But it was *really* bad when *Dad* got there, because everything seemed to just erupt as all the violence and outrage came to a head.

They were trying to get to him, and they were throwing things at him, and only the police kept them back. The police were just super everywhere we went. Of course, Dad is supported by the police nearly everywhere.

Rocks were thrown that just missed him, he was spit on, and one man just two persons away from him pulled a knife. One of the security men whirled around in his direction and the man ran off.

But Dad is the coolest person imaginable going through a crowd of people like that, because it affects him in no way at all. He calmly wiped the spit off and continued on his way.

Just as Dad came into the back door, which was up a small flight of steps, a piece of wood a foot long and three inches thick sailed past him through the door, barely missing several people. It hit the wall inside and bounced right down the center of the floor.

I looked at Dad, and the expression on his face was still just as calm as could be. He went into a little room to rest for ten minutes before his speech, his composure remaining completely unruffled, and as I watched him in amazement, he chatted with people as though nothing had happened. I thought it was just unbelievable.

In fact, I forgot that I was due to precede him on stage. And while I was standing around back there, they introduced me over the loudspeaker. And I didn't hear the introduction. So they introduced me again. And someone came running in and said, "They've introduced you!"

I didn't have my guitar on; it was in the case. So I grabbed the case and unsnapped it, and grabbed my "axe" and barely got my strap on as I ran up on the stage. Everybody laughed and thought it was funny that I was late. But I just told them I was talking to the Governor, and they understood.

The audience was friendly, unlike the crowd in the back of the auditorium. As usual, it was my function to break the ice before Dad came on and help warm the people up to a pitch of enthusiasm. It was very different from appearing at a club or dance, where I was on the bill and people knew what to expect. But these rallies were great experience for me nonetheless, and they enabled me to spend more time with my father.

My main concern at the rallies was always for him, especially when he was going through a crowd. I was well aware of what had happened in the past to others, and what was possible.

But although there was always danger for him, especially because he's so controversial, it didn't affect his behavior in the campaign. Nor has it affected his appearances since he was shot.

His mastery at handling crowds, even if they are hostile, was well-illustrated at a college in Michigan in 1972. He spoke in a large campus hall where people sat on the floor and in an upstairs balcony.

When we arrived, we found that over half the people who had pushed their way to the front of the downstairs section were against Dad and were there not necessarily to heckle him but to be very apathetic about what he had to say.

For my part, to know that I had to go out and play to that kind of audience was pretty disheartening. They had already decided they were against us. But the other musicians and I got through it. I was really worried, though, about how Dad would do. At the previous three or four rallies in Michigan, people had been stomping their feet and were really for him. So I didn't know what to expect.

But, as always, he handled it like a pro. Instead of a fire-and-brimstone speech like he usually gives, and they're great, he calmly lectured to the students on where he was and what he wanted to do.

It was really like going to a class in political science, and it was just the perfect thing to do. By the end of the speech I won't say they were all *for* him, but they were more receptive and I think they understood and appreciated him more. They even applauded politely.

For they saw he was well-read and intelligent and knew a lot about government, and that he believed in what he was saying. That was a perfect example of his reading a crowd and reacting to it effectively.

I stood in the wings and watched him, and my spirits soared.

I wandered outside, where it was cold and snowing.

And I talked to some students out there who were for my dad. They said they had organized a Young People for Wallace group just a few days earlier on the campus.

But I'm glad my father really reached those students inside with his speech. I think if you could go straight to the core of George Wallace you'd learn what he sees ahead for this country if a new direction is not taken. Hopefully our new President, Gerald Ford, is steering us in that direction. But now that so much power is stored up in the Presidency as shown by the Watergate scandal, Dad wants more than ever to return the power to the people, to the average man, and to bring people together. That's the only way to survive as a nation, he feels.

The crowds nearly everywhere were large and enthusiastic in Dad's 1972 campaign. Very few times did many people come to heckle. Dad trusted his security, and although much was written about his portable bullet-proof podium, he was constantly leaving it to mingle with the people who had come to see him. For he's the kind of man who has to meet the people individually as much as possible. Direct person-to-person contact is something he's got to have, and in any future campaigns he'll be the same way: he won't stay behind his podium.

At one point in 1972 someone thought of having him wear a bullet-proof vest. Had he worn it, he might be walking today. But it was too heavy and bulky for him to get around in easily, so he decided against it. He was always very fast with the crowds as he went through them meeting people and shaking hands.

He didn't even react when some people started throwing things at him at a few shopping centers in Maryland in early May. Colonel Dothard held his hands up to protect Dad from stones, eggs and vegetables, but Dad kept right on through the crowds, ignoring the danger.

And then, one night in May while we were campaigning in Maryland, I dreamed that my father was shot. In my dream, he was shot in the throat and died. I woke up shaking and upset.

Then we flew to Michigan for a day or two. And I mentioned my dream to Cornelia that Saturday when we were on the plane flying back to Montgomery for the Mother's Day weekend, because she had said something at one time about the interpretation of dreams, and I wanted to know what she thought my dream meant. And she was shocked.

She mentioned my dream to Dad, but of course it didn't affect his plans in any way.

After we arrived in Montgomery, I drove up to the University of Alabama to pick up some clothes I needed from the apartment I still maintained there. I was planning to go to Los Angeles for a few days to record.

On Monday afternoon, May fifteenth, I was in the apartment, lying on my bed and resting. Dad and Cornelia had already returned to Maryland for a final round of campaigning before the next day's primary. Catherine Motlow, a girl I was dating at the university, was watching television in the other room.

All at once she rushed through the door into the bedroom. I had been half-asleep, but her sudden entrance startled me and I was now fully awake.

She stood there with a blank, shocked expression on her face, and she said, "Your daddy's been shot!"

Chapter Thirteen

I LOOKED at Catherine for a second and then said, "Well, that's not funny."

And she just stood there with the same expression, very stunned. Because I don't think even *she* believed what she'd heard on television. I hadn't heard it, because the TV volume was down low.

And then she said it again: "Your daddy's been shot!" By that time *I* had heard it on television, so I jumped up and just stood there for a minute. My first thought was, had he been shot in the head?

Then I walked into the other room to hear the bulletins as they came over the TV every few minutes with the latest reports on the shooting. I was numb with fear and worry, and I hardly moved.

Within a very few minutes, there was a knock on the door and it was three state troopers. They told me they had already contacted the Governor's office in Montgomery and had made arrangements to fly me to Maryland. They were there to take me to the plane.

My friend, Dickie Whitaker, arrived at the apartment and he and Catherine joined us for the drive to the airport.

By then the TV announcer had reported that Dad had not been shot in the head—that there were abdominal wounds and a shoulder wound. From the moment I heard that there was no head injury, I never thought for a minute that my father would die.

I walked outside and to the right, where there was a swimming pool. People were standing all around the fence, just looking at my apartment, alarm written on their faces. They stared at me in horror as I passed. They couldn't believe what they'd heard. Some of them mumbled their regrets to me.

We hurried into the first of two state trooper cars, and the two cars rushed toward the airport at 90 or 95 miles an hour.

All the way to the airport, the knowledge that Dad had not been shot in the head helped me keep my composure. I just didn't think he would die.

And then a report came over the radio that his heart had stopped beating. That shattered my confidence, and my spirits sank. But then another report came on that he was still alive.

At the airport we had to wait about ten minutes for the plane to get there. There was really nothing any of us could say to each other.

And then the airplane arrived—an Aero Jet Commander, a state plane. Peggy Sue came out and ran up to me. She was very upset and threw her arms around me. I comforted her as best I could and we boarded the plane. The priority flight had originated in Montgomery with Peggy and some others aboard and had stopped at Tuscaloosa to pick me up.

Colonel Dothard's wife was also on the plane. The Colonel was Dad's security chief in Maryland and had also been shot. A bullet had passed through his stomach, but it was primarily just a flesh wound and we knew he was not in serious condition. So although Peggy and I were worried about Dad, we tried to reassure Mrs. Dothard about her husband's condition as we flew toward Washington. I think we all managed to hold each other together, because we were all in the same situation. Each had a loved one who'd been shot. I might add that I prayed a lot on that flight.

All other planes were routed out of our way and we soon reached Dulles International Airport outside Washington. We left the plane and hurried into the terminal, surrounded by security men. Newsmen approached us, but *I* wasn't going to talk to anybody, and neither was Peggy. We just wanted to get to the hospital. We could hear a TV newsman telling his viewers, "The Governor's children are going into the airport terminal." Then we were rushed out to a Secret Service car for the trip to Holy Cross Hospital in Silver Spring, Maryland, where they had taken Dad. The car was part of a police motorcade.

Our security on the whole trip from Alabama to Maryland was heavy, because—face it. Dad had been shot, and at that point in time no one knew what was going on, and whether all the members of his family were in danger. Was it a conspiracy? No one knew.

And do they now? *I* don't. But I have my suspicions.

My sister Peggy has her own memories of that day, of course. When we discussed it later she recalled, "When we got to the hospital it was just unbelievable—mass confusion! There were people all over the hospital grounds, and ABC, CBS and NBC trucks everywhere. They had their cameras aimed at the hospital. It was night by then, but it was like daytime because of the TV lights.

"And the security was so tight that when we drove up they told us, 'Can we have identification?' You said, 'Aw, man!' because you wanted to get into the hospital so badly.

"So that triggered *me,* and I don't remember what I said, but it must have been something obscene. And you told me, 'Peggy, don't *say* that! That's his job. He has to do his job.'

"When you said that, I thought, 'George, how can you think that when it's our father?' But as I said, you're so calm all the time. You were even calm on the plane.

"Then the driver, who was a security man, said, 'These are the Governor's children.' So they let us pass by and go into the hospital, where the lobby was so crowded that you couldn't even walk. They had to rope it off. And reporters were even going into hospital rooms where patients were lying in bed, and using their phones to call in stories."

Dad was still in surgery on the fifth floor when we arrived, undergoing a very long operation to remove one of the bullets, explore the extent of the damage and sew up the wounds. We were taken to a nearby nurses' lounge where we would wait with Cornelia, who was already there. Within a half hour, Bobbi Jo and Lee had joined us, having flown in together on a jet that brought Bobbi Jo from Birmingham and stopped in Montgomery for Lee. Both girls were fairly calm, but the whole family was still in a state of disbelief, really.

I wouldn't say that Cornelia was hysterical, but she was close. For after all, she had been with Dad when he was shot. Yet it was Dad who consoled *Cornelia* on the ambulance trip to the hospital. Later, however, she recovered her composure beautifully before going on television to reassure the nation that Dad would recover.

Fortunately she had not been injured at all during the assassination attempt despite her closeness to Dad at the time—unlike Colonel Dothard, who recently told me the traumatic details of what it was like to be shot with George Wallace.

"The Governor had only made one other speech that day, and that was in the parking lot at the Wheaton shopping plaza," recalled Colonel Dothard, who was a captain at the time of the shooting. "In a shopping center, people are inclined to have access to eggs and oranges and apples, and they did. They had everything, and they *threw* everything at the Governor.

"But nothing ever hit him at Wheaton. Matter of fact, somebody gave me one of those plastic signs, and I doubled it to keep the eggs and the rocks and the glass and everything away, and he was never touched.

"And when we got to the second stop, Laurel, Maryland, somebody had gone further and they had put cardboard in the sign and taped it, which made it a little stronger.

"After all the trouble at the first place, we fully expected to have the same thing at the second because it was a very short distance away.

"But it was fine at first—not a thing thrown. The crowd was friendly. I'd say 98 percent of them were *with* the Governor. They applauded.

"We had a few hecklers in back. We had a few black people that in a good humor would yell things and then they'd laugh, you know? But we didn't object to that at all, as long as they were *friendly* and not *throwing* things!"

They had arrived at the Laurel shopping center at 3:15, and the crowd in the parking lot numbered some 2,000. Billy Grammer and his three sidemen had warmed up the crowd with such songs as *Gotta Travel On* and *Detroit City*. Then, as Billy played *Dixie* on his electric guitar, Dad had appeared on the specially-erected stage.

He greeted the crowd with his usual "Hi, folks!" and then launched into a fifty-minute speech.

He ended by advising the audience to vote in the next day's Democratic primary "to shake the eyeteeth of the Democratic party. Let's give 'em the St. Vitus dance. And tell 'em a vote for George Wallace is a vote for the average citizen."

This was greeted with thunderous applause, and Dad was so encouraged that when he came off the stand he signed two or three pictures and then declared, "I believe I'll shake hands." He took off his jacket and handed it to an assistant because it was a hot day. Cornelia followed him into the crowd.

"Had he gone into the crowd at the first stop?" I asked Colonel Dothard.

"No! No! Not at all!" the Colonel assured me. "We would have objected *very* much to his going into *that* crowd. And if we had thought that maybe he shouldn't have done it in Laurel, we would have said something. And chances are he would have done what we asked.

"But Jim Taylor and I—Jim was in charge of the Secret Service—we looked at each other, and we didn't object, because there was no *reason* to object. We didn't have any threats. Nothing had been thrown. And it looked like a good place.

"So, to have some system to it, we decided to walk all the way around the ropes and back past the speaker's stand, and then he'd be at the car.

"And it was just like it was *everywhere* at a Wallace speech. He seems to generate some sort of electricity, and they all wanted to shake hands. And he was a past master at shaking with *both* hands. We'd just move down the rope, people pushing and shoving like they did everywhere and saying, 'Let *me* shake your hand.'

"And he'd gotten almost down to where the rope turned to come across in front of the speaker's stand. He moved to the right and moved to the left, shaking with both hands. And I always stay on the Governor's left. I've done that for so many years I could anticipate what he would do. If I heard a voice telling him to come back and he glanced that way, I knew that he was going back there. Then I could prepare to step back to the left and let him do it. And a lot of people called him back that day."

"Did Arthur Bremer call him back?" I asked Colonel Dothard.

"Well, there's been speculation that he said, 'I want to shake hands with you.' But he didn't call him back, because we hadn't gotten to him yet.

"The Governor kept shaking with both hands. And then, before we got down to Bremer—and the picture shows that Bremer was still to the right of Jim Taylor, who was on the *Governor's* right—he pushed the pistol through and fired the five shots.

"On the first shot I thought, 'Somebody's throwing

firecrackers.' We'd had *those* before. Then the dirt and the dust flew up, and the other four shots sounded like an automatic. And I knew what had happened.

"The first shot hit the Governor. And *I've* always believed that the second shot hit *me,* because we were both falling at the same time. He was falling straight back, and I was falling at an angle. But as *he* fell back, *I* was falling and I could see him. And I could see him even as we both struck the ground."

Arthur Bremer's snub-nosed revolver had hit Dad with four or five .38-caliber bullets. Two of them apparently passed through his right arm and shoulder, while one glanced off his left shoulder blade. Another burst through his abdomen, tearing open his stomach and nicking his large intestine.

The bullet that crippled him entered his spinal canal and stopped in the spinal fluid, pointing downward near the first lumbar vertebra, at his waist.

Cornelia, who had been near Dad, had paused to shake hands and chat with a woman, or she might have been shot, too. She bent over Dad as soon as he was hit and instinctively tried to shield his body with her own until help came.

As Dad lay on the ground, "he didn't look startled. He didn't look shocked," Colonel Dothard told me. "It had happened. I guess after you've been in this business as long as *he* has and you get all sorts of threats, your children are threatened, you say, 'Well, it's finally happened.'

"As a matter of fact, he had a very *calm* look on his face. I've mentioned that several times to my wife, about how calm he looked. He didn't look startled at all. He never lost consciousness, never lost his color.

"I *know* he never lost consciousness," Colonel Dothard emphasized. "One of the young agents pulled his pistol and kneeled down, and the Governor said, 'Don't *point* that at me.' I don't think the agent was, but it shows the Governor was still alert to the danger in a gun like that. And the agent *could* have cocked it in the excitement and it could have gone off.

"By then they'd already subdued Bremer. But I never did see Bremer—never did see his pistol.

"Although the Governor remained so calm, I'm sure he was scared. *I* was scared, and I'm sure *he* was. But you'd never have known it."

"What do you think about when you've just been shot?" I asked Colonel Dothard.

"All you know is that you've had the breath knocked out of you, and you're in a lot of pain and don't know the extent of your injury. And it's even worse when you've been involved in law enforcement like I have and you know that a stomach wound is the worst possible place to get shot.

"And of course the Governor's over there—you can see him. And he has on a light blue shirt. You can see all the blood on his right arm and on his stomach because the shirt is so light."

Also injured was Secret Service Agent Nicholas Zarvos, who was shot in the throat—which reminded me of my dream about Dad being shot in the throat. And Dora Thompson, one of my father's campaign workers, fell to the ground with a bullet in her right leg.

"It must have been a scene of panic," I said.

"It was, for a minute. And then the Secret Service and all of *our* people performed, I thought, *real* well.

They kept the crowd back and got a station wagon up there and had actually loaded the Governor in it when the ambulance came. And then they took him out of it and put him in the ambulance. They were *very* efficient.

"Before he was put in the ambulance, he asked Mrs. Wallace about me. He wanted to know how I was. And he looked at me in the ambulance. I was on a stretcher just like he was.

"There were twelve people in that little ambulance!" Colonel Dothard marveled. "Mrs. Wallace was by the Governor. Someone was holding me on the stretcher because we were going around the turns, and I asked him how fast we were going. He looked and said, 'Ninety-five miles an hour.' With twelve people!"

"Wasn't the unit that picked you up one of the best in the country?" I asked.

"Evidently so," he agreed. "They were well equipped and they knew their business.

"At one time the Governor said he had difficulty breathing and they gave him oxygen. But there was no way to tell whether he was in pain, because he never, never said a word *about* it. He never said, 'I'm hurting,' or 'I'm in pain.' The only things he said that I recall were, once or twice, 'How long till we get to the hospital?' and 'I'm having difficulty breathing.'"

The ambulance trip to Holy Cross Hospital took twenty-five minutes. "We were fortunate in that they had a good hospital, and it was a time of day, the middle of the afternoon, when a lot of doctors who ordinarily worked there were still there. And they had enough time to get other doctors who lived in the area.

"Corporal Hilyer of our state troopers stayed in

the operating room all during the Governor's surgery, and he says he was completely surrounded by doctors—all specialists.

"I was released while the Governor was still in surgery. The bullet had just passed through the fleshy part of my stomach. I never had any infection and in about six weeks my wound had healed completely.

"But the Governor had a real tough time, and I think he would have died, but he's always been strong physically," Colonel Dothard noted.

Yet at the time the doctors were operating on my father nothing was certain. "As we waited in the nurses' lounge for word on how he was, we realized from the expressions and the talk that he could die on the operating table," Peggy remembers.

The doctors did a wonderful job of keeping us informed on Dad's condition while he was in surgery, and later. They would talk to us individually or as a family and tell us how he was doing. If there was a setback at any time, they were completely honest with us. They removed the bullet from his abdomen and performed an exploratory operation to survey the extent of internal damage. But the bullet in his spine, which had caused the paralysis, was not removed until some days afterward. It had not only cost him the use of his legs; he had also lost control of his bowel and bladder functions.

Cornelia recently told me, "I was anxious to hear when the surgery was going on what kind of damage he had internally. You know—where the bullets had hit.

"I knew about the *paralysis* as soon as we got to the hospital," she added. "I was in the room when they were examining him. They stuck pins in him.

"I know a little bit about neurology, so when they stick pins in you and you don't say 'Oh!' then they know you don't have any feeling. So I *knew* he had no feeling and was paralyzed.

"First they asked him to move his legs, and he didn't. And I said, 'Well, you know, the Governor's deaf. I'm sure he didn't hear you.' And then they got the pins out. And when they got the pins out, I knew *exactly* what it meant."

I asked Cornelia, "Did you think even when he had no feeling in his legs that he might recover their use?"

"No, I didn't. I did not," she admitted. "When I knew he didn't have any feeling in his legs, I didn't think he would.

"I *always* thought he would *live*," she emphasized. "I mean, he *talked* all the way to the hospital, he talked till they put him to sleep in the surgery. He was aware, he was alert. He was talking about different things. He never lost consciousness, and his injuries were all low.

"He didn't have any apparently fatal wounds that I could detect. If he'd had some major artery severed, he would have bled so much he'd have passed out.

"The thing I didn't think about was the spleen and a few other organs that the bullet went all around. They thought he had liver damage. But even if his liver had been shot half off, you know, they'd have taken it out, repaired it and stitched it back up, and then it would have regenerated. So *that* wouldn't have been a fatal thing.

"He had five hours of surgery beginning about four o'clock, and then they brought him to the recovery room after nine o'clock," Cornelia recalled.

Peggy remembers, "When they brought him into the recovery room, we went in. And of course you stayed very calm, George. He was still sedated heavily, but he was in so much pain, and the arm he got shot in was just un- believable. I had never seen a gunshot wound before, and the arm was this big across—about eight inches—I mean, like a balloon!

"And Cornelia said, 'The children are here, and I'm here.' And she named all of our names, remember?"

I nodded. It had been eerily like Mother's dying moments, when Dad had told her we were there and named each one of us. I recalled, "Even though he was in terrible pain, he recognized us all and reached for our hands. And he said, 'How y'all?' He was very pale, because he'd lost quite a bit of blood. But he looked *great* to me at that point. He looked fantastic, because he was alive!"

Peggy remembered, "We could only stay a few seconds in the recovery room—a room they had set up just for him—and then we went back to the nurses' lounge. We stayed there two or three hours, till they took him up to intensive care, and then we all went up with him."

But first, while Dad was in the recovery room, Cornelia went on television to tell the nation that Dad would be all right. She spoke in a makeshift press room after he came out of surgery, and the family members were with her.

"The reason I went on television was that there were a lot of people around that really shouldn't have been back there," Cornelia told me. "Frankly, nobody should have been in that area but the Governor's family. None of his staff should have been there. But you have people who want to be around you and comfort you.

"Well, some of them thought George— It was like they were *mourning* him. And he wasn't even dead! I really got angry about the whole thing, because their attitude was such that *they* didn't cheer me up.

"I mean, *I* had the faith. I believed he was going to

be all right. I just wanted to know how bad his injuries were. I *never* thought he would die.

"There was a priest there that was praying, the sisters were there, and *they* were giving me the kind of *spiritual* comfort I needed. But I didn't need people with long faces mourning somebody when I had hope. I had faith. And the longer we waited for the surgery to be over, the more these people were trying to *bury* him. It was just awful. And it made me angry that they didn't have any more faith than that.

"So I knew that if those people at the hospital were worried that he would die, I just *knew* that all the people that cared about him at home and all over the country, all the masses of people that loved George and cared about him—they would think the same thing.

"And I knew that when those doctors went out to give their report, if they'd give this technical stuff the people really wouldn't know that he was going to make it.

"So I thought, 'Well, if *I* say it, if I can go before those cameras and I'm composed enough—if they can hear it from me—I believe that it'll reassure them and give them the kind of faith that they need to believe that he's going to be all right.' So I told his press aide to set it up.

"But some of George's cohorts were determined that I should not go on. And they really kept me from going on at first, where I could have gone on as soon as his surgery was over. As soon as they told me that all of his organs were intact—that he had no fatal damage—nothing that could cause him any fatal-type outcome—then I wanted to go on."

"Why didn't they want you to go on?" I asked.

"I guess you'll have to ask them. Apparently they

thought I was going to do some *political* thing," she shrugged. "But it *insulted* me. Because I felt like *they* were not in any position to tell *me* what I should and should not do. Instead of *cooperating* with me and trying to make things *easy* for me, they made things more *difficult* for me. I was under *enough* strain, having an injured husband, without having to fight and struggle against these people.

"I thought they were making the arrangements. I'd ask and I'd ask, and finally—at least two hours after I'd told them—finally I told the Governor's press aide, Billy Joe Camp, who was *not* against my speaking, that either they'd set the thing up so I could go on or I was just going to go on out there to where the press were and *do* the thing.

"So when I was finally allowed to go on television, I just said that my husband had come out of surgery, and that the doctors would give them a medical briefing as soon as they could get over to the auditorium, and that I would not try to go into any kind of a medical report, because the doctors would cover that thoroughly. That's the reason I didn't mention the paralysis—because I knew there would be a lot of questions that I couldn't answer about it.

"So I just told them that my husband had all of his vital organs, that he was not injured in his spleen or his liver, and his head and heart were all sound . . . and that I couldn't thank God more for that.

"What I was trying to do was reassure all the people that had been waiting for news of George, but I felt it was a little late by then, because it was after the ten o'clock news and they would finally have turned off their sets and gone to bed."

Cornelia also said on TV that Dad would continue his

campaign—that he was not out of the race. And that's the way I'm sure he wanted it. If she hadn't said it, I would have, because I believe in him that much and I know what kind of man he is and what he wants to do.

After the broadcast, we saw Dad once more in intensive care. And he was still in great pain. By then I'd heard that he was paralyzed, but that was secondary in my thinking, because I was just relieved that his mind was all right. That had been my main concern.

However, even when he was shot and fell to the ground, he was alert. I found out later that he had shut his eyes for about twenty seconds, and that was quick thinking. Because if anybody else had been involved in the shooting, they would probably have thought that he was gone and wouldn't have shot him again. That was when he waited for the world to fade away if he was going to die.

That night Dad was given extremely heavy sedation so that he could get some sleep. The family stayed up most of the night at the hospital. They gave me a room, but I wasn't able to sleep much at all. Later in the morning we went to a motel and got a little rest.

We stayed at a Howard Johnson Motel a few miles away, and that became the family headquarters for some time. Nobody in the family left Maryland for at least ten days—not until Dad was out of danger. And Cornelia and Peggy were there for over a month, until Dad left the hospital. During that period, Peggy left town only long enough to take her college finals at Troy State University in Alabama, then she returned to Maryland.

Cornelia says admiringly of Peggy, "She stayed at the hospital with me and she stayed in my motel room and went back and forth, and she and I sat together like a vigil for I don't know how many weeks. We were at the hospital every day and every night, and it got to the point where almost in order to get her out I had to go to the Sonny and Cher show with her."

The morning after he was shot, when Dad woke up one of his first questions was about Colonel Dothard's condition.

"But I had already come home," the Colonel told me. "I took the same plane back to Montgomery that had brought the family up.

"When the Governor asked about me, they said, 'He's fine. He's gone.' I don't think he *believed* them, because *he* didn't know what shape I was in. I think they had a pretty tough time convincing him that I was all right and had actually gone home."

Although he was still in great pain that day, Dad's resiliency was so amazing that he jokingly asked one of his aides: "What have you got me scheduled for today?"

And on that same day, Dad won the Presidential primaries in Maryland and Michigan by wide margins.

In Maryland he received 39 percent of the vote. Sen. Hubert Humphrey received 27 percent, and Sen. George McGovern won 22 percent.

In Michigan he won an even greater victory, taking 51 percent of the vote to 27 percent for McGovern and 16 percent for Humphrey.

These triumphs raised his morale tremendously. And the day after the elections Dad felt strong enough to pose for press photos holding a newspaper that headlined his primary victories, with Cornelia by his side.

Although he had not previously arranged for extensive campaigns in any of the later primaries, he eventually won some 400 delegate votes that year.

My first lengthy visit with Dad following the shooting took place several days after he was injured, while he was still in intensive care.

He was behind a plate glass window, and I could see him through the glass from the hall. I was sitting there one day. I had seen him several times, but we'd had no conversation because he was quite weak. He was being fed intravenously and had lost a lot of weight.

As I sat there watching him, he looked over and motioned for me to come in. It wasn't really a conversation, but he took my hand and turned his head and shut his eyes. I stood there for twenty minutes holding his hands until he went to sleep. But I feel my dad and I can communicate without words a lot of times. I think we're that close.

Having his family nearby really raised Dad's morale. So did the mail and telegrams and phone calls he received at the hospital. They were bringing in four or five large sacks of mail a day, and there were so many letters that Dad couldn't read them all. In Silver Spring he read mostly telegrams, which I'd look at first and hand to him. And I answered many of the phone calls. He did look through the letters when he returned to Montgomery, and it gave him great inspiration to know that so many people still had confidence in him.

As you know, several top Democratic politicians came to the hospital to see him. In fact, Senator Humphrey, who was in the state at the time of the shooting, had gone to the hospital immediately to console Cornelia.

After my first silent but meaningful visit with Dad in intensive care, I would go in to see him and ask him how he was feeling, and he'd assure me, "I'm doing fine."

He always encouraged *us*. He's that kind of guy. When he's down, he's worried about everybody else.

When he found out I'd be going to New Mexico and California to campaign for him about two weeks after he was shot, he warned me, "Son, just be careful." Because I'm sure the thought was in his mind that anything could happen. As long as he knew his family was all right, he wasn't too concerned about himself.

In New Mexico we had a press conference in Albuquerque. Charlie Snyder, the head of the national campaign, was with me. And I felt he could best answer questions about campaign strategy.

My role was really just to assure people how well Dad was getting along—that he was really recovering.

Since I as his son was doing all that traveling, people could realize, "Well, if his son can travel for him he doesn't have to stay by his bedside, so he's getting along better." And he was indeed doing well by the time I was in New Mexico.

I went to California and did several television shows, including "The Merv Griffin Show," "Tempo" and "The George Putnam Show," and had a press conference at my hotel. Dad saw me on the Griffin show while he was in the hospital in Maryland, and when I got back he told me he was very proud of me. But he's not one to heap praise on you. He feels the job is there to be done and there's nothing to do but *do* it. That's the way he himself has lived.

In addition to my California appearances, where my job again was to assure people that Dad was recovering, I did a fund-raising rally in Lakeland, Florida, on a farm owned by George Jones and Tammy Wynette, the country music stars. Ferlin Husky, Melba Montgomery and several other artists were there. I was asked to sing, but at that point I didn't really think I should be singing, so I just spoke on the stage, thanking the people of Florida for the confidence they had expressed in Dad. His primary victories that year began in Florida. I had no problem talking, because I could feel the compassion people had for him, and my words came from my heart. In addition to my speech, I answered questions about Dad. And then I went through the audience, shaking hands. Women would start to cry when they greeted me, because they really had that much feeling for Dad.

Six weeks after the shooting, the Democratic National Convention was held in Miami. And Dad was there to address the convention.

President Nixon sent an Air Force hospital plane to take Dad to Miami. I boarded the plane when it stopped in Montgomery and flew on to Florida with Dad, Cornelia and Peggy.

There was a tremendous crowd at Dannelly Field in Montgomery when the plane landed there on its way to the convention. Dad got off the plane and they rolled him up to a podium, and he spoke to the crowd. He got a little choked up because of what he'd been through and because he was so emotional about finally being back home. He knew these were his people, and that they had come to see him and wish him well.

He told them he was recovering rapidly and he thanked them for their thoughts and prayers, their calls and letters—and he assured them that the campaign wasn't over yet.

On the plane to Miami, I sat by him for awhile, and although we didn't say too much, from what he told me I could tell that his head was full of politics and strategies as always. And that showed me he was really recovering. He had an air of great concentration about him as he planned for his appearance before his fellow Democrats. He knew they'd be watching him intently and listening to him closely to see whether George Wallace was indeed still a force to be reckoned with on the national scene.

In Miami we stayed at the Four Ambassadors Hotel and held a series of receptions for delegates from the various states. They all marveled at how well Dad was doing. Just his being there showed a lot of people how much he had improved. His weight was down considerably, but he was regaining his strength. And mentally he had never lost any of his sharpness at all, even though he was in constant pain then and for a year afterward.

He tried to handle a lot of the pain without drugs, to preserve his mental acuteness and to avoid the danger of addiction, either physical or psychological.

And yet he could joke about the subject. One time when the pain was particularly bad, he did want an injection for it but nobody was around to give it to him at the moment. He said wryly, "I can call out the National Guard, but I can't get a shot."

Much of the pain at first had come from an infection caused by his abdominal wound, but there was considerable pain even after the infection cleared up, because of his spinal injury. (Ironically, the abdominal infection had been largely caused by a hamburger he had eaten an hour before he was shot. The bullet had torn through his intestines and sent the food throughout his abdominal cavity, and the normal bacteria in the food started the infection, causing abscesses which had to be drained until they could be cleared up.)

The delegates couldn't tell he was in pain except when he occasionally gripped his side. He never mentioned it.

And when he addressed the convention, where he was cheered by most delegates but booed by a few, he was in so much control of himself that nobody knew he was in pain at all. He's not one to feel sorry for himself, and he detests having anyone else feel sorry for him.

Of course, he rested as much as he could in Miami, and he was undergoing physical therapy at times. His therapy had started just before he left Holy Cross Hospital. A doctor from Spain Rehabilitation Clinic, which is located at the University of Alabama's Birmingham Medical School, was in charge of his therapy at Miami, along with two nurses who had come from Holy Cross. But even though he went through his therapy daily, he was so concerned with the convention that it was hard for him to concentrate on it in Miami.

From Miami Dad flew to Spain Rehabilitation Clinic in Birmingham, where he had minor abdominal surgery to further clear up his wounds and underwent rigorous therapy for a month. Upon his return to Montgomery he continued the therapy in a bedroom he had specially outfitted for that purpose at the Mansion, and he is continuing it to this day. In addition to walking on a treadmill between parallel bars with braces on his legs, balancing himself as he walks, he lies on his back on a slanted board and lifts heavy weights which are mounted on large rubber wheels so that he can't injure himself if they should fall. He also has his legs and feet bent and massaged to strengthen the muscles and ligaments. His legs were undersized for awhile, but as a result of the exercises they are now filled out.

While he was in Birmingham, Dad received thousands of letters at the Mansion congratulating him on his speech at the Miami convention. He read many of these on his return to Montgomery and they helped raise his morale at a time when he was in need of a psychological boost.

His campaign was over, the convention was past, he had finished the intensive therapy at Spain Rehabilitation Clinic, and now he was home and to a large degree on his own, settling into the routine of being a paralytic with tremendous personal adjustments to make while still running the state.

For a few months it was quite a blow to him mentally that he couldn't walk. He was fifty-three years old and had led such an active, athletic life, really energetic—and suddenly he was crippled.

I could see the depression, and I'm sure others in the family could. But he wouldn't let anybody *else* see it. Not at the office, and not in public.

How did I sense his depression? Well, for a while he was reminiscing about the past a great deal—about his political career, the campaigns, and he talked about Clayton a lot, and about Clio—about Barbour County, where he was born and raised.

And it dawned on me one day that he was thinking about the past *so much,* when he should be thinking about the future as he had always done. Because the past has its place, but you've got to look toward tomorrow.

So we tried to get him out of it, Cornelia and the rest of us. We tried not to *cater* to him—not to treat him like an invalid. Not that he had wanted us to, but we had found ourselves *doing* that, because we hated to see him in that shape.

But we began to think, "Hey, we've got to help him pull himself out of this and *center* himself again."

I don't know how much *we* did to help him, because I think he's such a strong person that he's always a step ahead of everybody. So I believe he figured it out too, and gradually he stopped reminiscing and his depression seemed to pass. Not that he'd given up *ever,* but he'd been dwelling on his past life and on the fact that now he was paralyzed. I'm sure anyone would do that. And I think there are probably a lot of people who would *still* be in that shape.

When did I first notice that his mood was changing for the better? Well, I would go in and see him a lot, and I would just sit by him while he'd rest or sleep. And gradually he seemed to perk up. But I think I started noticing it more on the phone.

The first time I detected it, I had gone somewhere for the weekend and I called him to see how he was doing. And he sounded like he had before he was hurt. His voice was strong again.

I'll tell you when I could *really* be sure that he was better. It was when he'd get on me for something small—I think probably when he started mentioning again that I ought to cut my hair.

He used to kid me about it in an *affectionate* way, really, because he doesn't dislike someone with long hair, and mine is not that long anyway.

But when he started kidding me about my hair again, I realized he was feeling better. So I'd start joking with him. I'd say, "Well, hey—I've told several people that *you're* going to grow a *mustache.* So you've got to do it, or make me out a liar!" And he would laugh, so I knew he was improving. But he'd never promise to grow one. He kept his options open!

Then he started to *look* better, and he began gaining weight. His muscle tone improved and his upper body eventually was in superb shape.

He's more muscular than ever now, and his right hand is *very* strong. The other day in his therapy room he told me, "Son, see those weights over there? Go pick 'em up."

I said, "For what?" I was just kidding with him, because he'd been bench pressing them all day on his back. I said, "*I* don't want to pick those things up!"

And he said, "Aw, *you* can probably lift more than *me*, you know?" So he'd gotten his humor back. And he was smiling a lot more.

However, the year 1972 was a difficult one for *all* the Wallaces, including Dad's mother, Mozelle. And I want to mention her here before going on.

"I had brain surgery on the 10th of April in 1972," Mozelle recalls. "All my children were right there when I needed them. George cut off all his campaigning and his state duties to be with me.

"Then I had only been home a few weeks from the hospital when he was shot. When it happened, I just went into a state of shock. I couldn't realize it!

"But I had *always* felt that—sooner or later—something would happen. Because that's in every mother or wife's mind if her loved one is running for office. She always has that anxiety about him.

"So—it was a blow. And I couldn't be with him afterward, because it took me about seven or eight months to get over my operation. My doctor wouldn't let me go out of town. So I didn't see him until he came home.

"But I'd talk to him on the phone, and he'd say, 'I'm going to be all right. I'm going to be all right.' And after a certain length of time we *all* felt he would be. It was just the first twenty-four or forty-eight hours that we were most apprehensive.

"Somebody else might have given up. But he has always had a determination to fight. And he had good doctors and nurses who supervised his progress and encouraged him with his therapy.

"I don't believe George would have gotten this far in his recovery if he hadn't made the effort to do all the things he had to, when he was in so much pain," Mozelle observed.

"You know, when he was taking all the therapy in Birmingham he was feeling a *lot* of pain. And sometimes he'd say, 'Well, I hurt so bad I don't want to do anything.' But he's made a good comeback.

"*I* just believe *someday* George is going to *walk* again," Mozelle concluded. "I may not live to see it, but— I really believe he's going to walk again."

Chapter Fourteen

ONE OF THE surgeons at Holy Cross Hospital told us that if it hadn't been for Dad's strong constitution he would probably have died.

This may well be true. But in my opinion Dad's life was primarily saved by his own faith, his will, his courage—call it his spirit, the combination of qualities that make up the man. You can't keep a man like George Wallace down.

This became evident as the months and years passed following his accident. We usually call it his accident when we discuss it in the family. We almost never mention Arthur Bremer, who was sentenced to sixty-three years in prison in August, 1972, in Upper Marlboro, Maryland, on four charges of assault with intent to murder and five charges of weapons-law violation. None of us feels any personal hostility toward him—not even my father. As for myself, I think he was just acting as part of a conspiracy. So how could I have any personal feelings about him?

For more than a year my father was never without pain, yet he never complained. For then, as always, he was a man with a mission.

I wish everyone could sit down and have a conversation with Dad, and see what he's all about—see the personal side of George Wallace. I hope this book is providing some insights into the man I know, and the man his friends and relatives know.

Juanita Halstead says, "George is just as charming as he can be—absolutely! I have seen people who opposed him politically talk to him for twenty or thirty minutes, and you could just *see* their animosity fading . . . sort of melting off. He talks so naturally to people that it just rings true.

"One evening I had a couple of women from North Carolina visiting me, and George was here," Juanita recalls. "And they had told me earlier that they did not admire him, they did not care for his philosophy and so forth. So I said, 'Well, he's going to be here tonight, and I'm sure you'll enjoy talking to him, whether you agree with him or not.'

"So, sure enough, after dinner they were still here and he came in and had a conversation with them. And I saw one of them just a few months ago, and she told me they've been for him ever since they met him!"

As for those who still hold Dad's past segregationist views against him, I would refer them to his brother, Gerald, who points out their historical context. "I don't really think that George knew at the time he made his 'Segregation now, segregation forever' speech that he would be any persuasive force on the national scene," says Gerald. "And of course integration and segregation was the question in the South at the time. And to be politically successful in the South, you had to take a stand one way or the other. He took a stand!

"His views today are just like everybody else's in the South. Those questions are gone—they're solved!" Gerald adds. "There's no more question of segregation in the South. That's a thing of the past. Nobody thinks about it any more."

I feel my father is a very compassionate man, and I don't think many people see that side of him. But a story from his youth helps illustrate what I mean.

It happened when he was fifteen or sixteen and was fighting for the Golden Gloves bantamweight championship. The night before a fight, he and his manager were walking down the street when they came upon two white fellows who were harassing a black who was much younger.

The white guys were a couple of years older than my dad and they each outweighed him by fifty or sixty pounds. But Dad ran up to them immediately and told them to leave the boy alone.

His manager tried to keep Daddy from intervening, because boxers are not supposed to get involved in a street fight of *any* kind. But all my dad could see at that point was a black boy being harassed. That's why he told them to let the boy go.

Before he even got the words out, one of the white boys had hit him and knocked him flat on his back. But he was up and knocked both of them out in less than a minute.

Some people may say, "Well, you're telling me that because it was a token effort on his part." But it wasn't. He saw someone being abused for no good reason, and he saved him. That's the perfect example of the way he is.

The people of Alabama understand the real George Wallace, and that's why they have allowed him to speak for them all over the country and have welcomed him back from each trip—and why they have voted for him time and again. They know that because of him the South and the State of Alabama are understood and respected as never before.

Through his efforts, other Americans began to see that the people of the South are *not* illiterates just because their speech may be a little slower. They may have a southern drawl, but their *minds* aren't any slower. They're basically good, decent people, and I think Dad has helped show that.

However, he's not very well liked among certain of the controlling interests in this country—some of whom were exposed by the Watergate inquiry.

Recalling the $400,000 in secret Republican campaign funds that had been sent into Alabama to help his Democratic opponent in 1970, he noted, "In a way, I am a victim of Watergate." But he hasn't been stopped. And he's really about the only voice the average American workingman *has*. Although he's not a rich man, he's honest to the core and can't be bought. The Internal Revenue Service has checked him several times and can *tell* you he has no hidden wealth.

He also believes in honesty in international affairs. He has always said that the Russians have never kept a treaty and they're never to be trusted. He wished President Nixon all the success possible when he visited China and Russia. But he's a great friend of Chiang Kai-shek and visited Taiwan during a trip to the Far East.

He would like to be friends with all foreign nations, but he thinks we need to stay strong militarily. That's the best deterrent to war. He's not for a fight, but he wants us to stay on our guard.

Despite his concern for state, national and international affairs, Dad has remained very interested in his family and what we're doing. In fact, as he has said, since his accident he feels closer to us than ever.

In the fall of 1972 Dad was continuing his steady progress toward recovery from his wounds, so I took advantage of a chance to tour as a performer with the Hank Williams, Jr., show for about six weeks, though I kept in close touch with the family by phone.

In fact, my Uncle Gerald became my manager in 1972, so that was another link between the family and my career. Gerald's guidance has been most valuable and has helped give my career direction.

Then, in 1973, through Buddy Lee, who had been booking my act, I met Mike Curb, then the president of MGM Records. Mike had heard some demonstration records of mine and had wanted to talk to me. His encouraging words gave me new confidence.

As a result of that meeting, I signed a contract with MGM Records, the first major company with which I had ever been associated. My first record was cut in Los Angeles. It was *Why Don't They Understand?* backed with *There'll Never Be Anyone Else But You.*

We had a press conference at the Jefferson Davis Hotel in Montgomery on June 16, 1973, to introduce the record. Mike Curb and other MGM executives and many members of the media were there. But what made me happiest was the fact that Dad appeared at the press conference, posed for pictures with me and with my record, and told the press how proud he was of me and how much he liked the record. It was a day I'll never forget.

That first record was played a lot on the radio but was not a big seller. It was partly country–western and partly middle of the road, so it was not a real hit in either area. But it helped make my music better known around the country and opened a lot of doors as far as television and personal appearances are concerned. I became more active in both areas.

I hate to label my music, though some might call it folk rock. What I do know is that I've become more interested in writing my own songs. If I couldn't write any of the songs I perform, I wouldn't want to stay in music. Although I wrote neither of the tunes on my first record, lately MGM has started letting me record my own songs, and this is much more fulfilling to me.

My sister, Peggy Sue, has mentioned that I keep my emotions under firm control and has said she wonders where I find my release.

Well, I put my emotions into my music. That's the only place I'm able to express them fully. I seem to be in a different world when I'm writing and playing my own songs.

So *music* is my release, and that is why it means so much to me. In music alone do I find my freedom.

Chapter Fifteen

WHEN I MOVED back into the Governor's Mansion in the fall of 1973 after having my own apartment for some months, the first night I was there I dreamed that my father walked.

And I believe there is something *to* that. I'm his only son, right? I think there is something psychic between us that I can't explain and he can't explain, but it's there.

I don't really know how much credit you can put in dreams and how you can explain them. But it made me feel good to dream that.

I've had other psychic feelings in regard to my father. Previously I mentioned my dream that he would be shot. But that's not all. When I was at the University of Alabama, before Dad was injured, he was pretty busy but he'd call me every two or three weeks. And when he did have a chance to call I was always very glad to talk with him.

Ever so often I'd get a feeling out of the blue that he was going to call, and he'd usually phone me that day. It would happen four out of five times, and it was strange. So I believe there *is* something to the psychic.

Not long after moving back into the Mansion, I was hospitalized for several days, suffering from a kidney stone. So I missed a very special event in Dad's life. His home town of Clio held a homecoming for him. My Uncle Jack, who attended with Dad, filled me in on it later.

"That was the first time Clio had ever had a homecoming for George, and we all went," Jack said. "They had most of the 1936 football team that he was captain of, and even the football coach, who came back from Mississippi to attend. It was just a real good day.

"George got there early, and we went over to the school lunchroom to eat. They had fried chicken and fried catfish for the public. We got there a little after 12, and I left about 3:15 or 3:30, and he was just getting away from the table. Everybody had to go through the line and get served so they went right by his seat. I think he shook *everybody's* hand . . . stopped and reminisced and talked to everybody . . . he was sitting there trying to eat for three hours.

"Later I was talking to Colonel Dothard, and he said, 'Well, I'll be glad when the boss can put in a full day.' And then he laughed and told me why he was saying that. He said he saw George going to Clio at 8 o'clock that morning, that he stayed at Clio till 4 or 5 o'clock, and he went from there to Troy State University for the dedication of a new Trojan Horse. I didn't see it, but I read later that it snorts red smoke when the team scores. And it snorted while George was standing in front of it, and it dyed his suit.

"But anyway, he was at *that* program, and then Dothard said that one of the security men told him that at

11:30 that night he was still out at the Garrett Coliseum at the horse show, shaking hands. And he'd been up since 6 o'clock that morning.

"It was just a week later that he went to the University of Alabama Homecoming," Jack added. "He participated in the pep rally the night before the game, and in the halftime festivities when he crowned the Homecoming Queen. That was when he made all the headlines because of the fact that she is black.

"So, judging from his schedule, he's doing just fine, I think," said Jack.

Yes, Dad really gets around. One day he went to the Fiddlers' Convention at Athens, Alabama, and played *Wildwood Flower* on the guitar . . . not very well, naturally.

In December, 1973, Peggy Sue married Mark Kennedy of Greenville, Alabama, who is a student at Cumberland Law School in Birmingham. The wedding was held at St. James Methodist Church in Montgomery, our family church, and the reception was in the Governor's Mansion.

People from all over the state crowded into the reception, and we were able to see friends we had not seen for a long time. Mark and Peggy took a good bit of kidding about having formed "the Kennedy-Wallace ticket," but they were used to that, having heard the joke all during their courtship. Mark is a really nice person, and we're all very happy to have him in the family. But no, he's not related to the "other" Kennedys.

In January, 1974, I enrolled at Huntingdon College in Montgomery, a school with only five hundred students but very high academic standards.

I had decided to attend Huntingdon instead of returning to the university for several reasons. Mainly I wanted to be near my father. Living in the Executive Mansion, I see him constantly.

I also wanted to be near my girl friend, Janice Culbertson, who was attending Huntingdon but has recently graduated. She has developed into a really accomplished painter and has had two art shows in Montgomery and one in Nashville.

But my reasons for attending Huntingdon College are not only personal. I like the college itself very much. I am majoring in history and minoring in political science, and I'm back in school to graduate. I even attended summer school in 1974 to pick up twelve extra hours. So I expect to graduate in a few months. And I'd like to go to law school.

Although I've talked about returning to college to help my father in his work someday, I decided on history instead of political science as my major because I've always been interested in history and because I talked at length to the head of the history department, Dr. Gordon T. Chappell, who really swayed me. And history, of course, gives you a better perspective on government.

When I first started classes, the other students really didn't know what I was going to be like. So I made a real effort to make friends and get involved in the college activities, and it's really one of the best things that could ever have happened to me. Because the standards are so high, most of the students there are really into what they're doing.

One unfortunate event complicated my life at Huntingdon for a while, but I adjusted to the situation quickly.

Because of the Patricia Hearst kidnaping, I had a security man assigned to accompany me around campus and sit outside my classrooms for two months in the spring of 1974.

The other students accepted it, however—that's the good thing. They understood, and were really good about it.

I was also fortunate that my security man was Sergeant Bud Watts of the state troopers, for he's an extremely intelligent and interesting man. He graduated from college and teaches constitutional law to other troopers at the academy in Montgomery. He also teaches firearms and karate. So he's a well-rounded, fascinating man, and we got to know each other well and became close friends.

In fact, Bud was a close friend of my mother's. They used to drink coffee together in the kitchen of the Governor's Mansion, which was significant, because anybody who drank coffee with her was a friend.

During my first semester in political science class I got a taste of teaching, and I liked it. I had a project that I presented to the class over a number of days. It had to do with the revision of our state constitution. I was a little nervous before I started, but I did a lot of research and really got into the subject, and I think the presentation came off very well. The students really enjoyed it, and I earned an A-plus for the project.

Last summer I took a philosophy class, and for a week I had to lead a discussion group. My particular subject, you may be surprised to learn, was civil disobedience and whether it can ever be justified.

I presented the views of various philosophers, and my own thoughts as far as the new generation is concerned.

I pointed out that with the young generation over

the past few years most of the civil disobedience has been on *moral* grounds—for a cause, rather than for pleasure or for publicity. They felt the moral obligation within themselves to show that a law was wrong.

You're probably asking, did George Wallace's son come out for civil disobedience? But I must tell you that I haven't really decided whether morality *is* a justification for breaking the law. I *have* learned through my studies and discussions on the subject that it's hard sometimes to bring the moral and the legal aspects together. And I have gained a greater understanding of those whose consciences have moved them to violate the law. I think that alone is significant as far as my own life is concerned.

Speaking of race relations, I found myself making some unexpected national headlines in that regard in the spring of 1974. I was even mentioned on the network television news.

And yet it all started very quietly as a sociology project at Huntingdon College.

The idea of the project was to see how people reacted in unexpected situations. To do this, our sociology class divided into groups, each of which was calculated to startle people in the community in a different way.

One group posed as female slaves offered for sale at $2,500 each in a shopping mall. Another group walked around with their faces painted green. And as my assignment, I teamed up with a black classmate named Evelyn Bradford. We pretended to be an interracial couple about to get married, and we visited several apartment complexes in Montgomery and asked if we could look at apartments.

To begin with, let me say this. The experiment was not accurately reported by Walter Cronkite on CBS-TV, or by the wire services, or by the nation's newspapers outside Montgomery.

It was reported nationally that out of four apartment complexes we went to, three turned us down and one did not. Well, that's not the case at all. *Nobody* turned us down.

At every apartment complex we visited, every resident manager we talked to showed us everything we wanted to see in the apartments and answered any questions we had.

I *would* say that two or three of the managers who showed us the apartments were a little—shall I say—surprised? Because, let's face it. You don't *see* that kind of thing every day in Alabama, although you may in other parts of the country.

So it was *new* to them. And it's hard to keep your expression from showing someone that it *is* new to you. But they showed us everything we wanted to look at, and they were just as courteous as they could be.

Of course, all of this interested Evelyn and me, because we were there to see people's reactions. But everyone was polite.

For instance, in a couple of apartment complexes we had to go through the pool section to see the apartments, and there were people sitting around the pools. And a couple of times we saw one or two people look up, but there was really no visible reaction on their faces.

Perhaps nobody but the people involved would have heard about the project, but a lady reported it for a local paper. The projects were done on a Friday, and she came to the college on Monday and wrote a little story as she always had with *all* the projects.

There was a little section in the story on each project,

and ours got no more coverage than anyone else's. But my name stood out and the other news media picked it up. It's too bad they didn't print the true story, as the lady who came to our class did. She printed what happened and what was said. But the others came out with things that didn't happen, things I didn't say, things I couldn't understand. And that really made me angry.

You may wonder whether it bothered me to go out and engage in a social experiment in which I pretended to be engaged to a black girl. It didn't bother me at all! *I* wanted to see for *myself* what the reactions or nonreactions would be. It was a learning experience for me, and that's how I regarded it. I *volunteered* to do it.

As far as the political consequences because of my being a member of George Wallace's family—and this happened during a primary election campaign in which he was running for reelection as Governor—I really can't say that I didn't consider them. Because I couldn't have grown up in this atmosphere *without* considering the political consequences of anything I might do.

But really, while I'm for my dad and believe in what he's doing, at the same time I have to consider *myself*— my own being, my own consciousness, what I'm aware of, and what I have to learn. And the only way I can do that is to experience things for myself. I have my own life to live.

So as far as I was concerned, I was just another student in an experiment. And of *course* the publicity was so great because of who I am and the position I'm in. But I *enjoyed* doing it, and it was really enlightening.

I didn't discuss it with my father or anyone else in the family in advance. It was a sociology project at the school, and I made the decision to do it. And after I had made my decision, I saw no need to consult anyone. Even after it happened and there was all that publicity, my father didn't say anything to me about it. Nothing at all.

Campaigning with my father in the 1974 Gubernatorial election was not really much different than it had been before. And the end result was the same as usual: he won.

He campaigned mostly on weekends for the May primary. I traveled with him, and sat on the stage while he spoke. After his speech he would sit in his wheelchair, either on or near the stage, and shake hands with all comers, while I moved into the crowd and shook hands with the people he could not reach as easily as he had in the past.

All the members of the family took part in the campaign, including Cornelia, Lee, Bobbi Jo and her husband, Jim Parsons, and the newlyweds, Peggy Sue and Mark Kennedy.

There had been a great deal of speculation that it would be hard for Dad to campaign in 1974. But if there was any question about his condition and his ability to travel all over the state, it was quickly erased. In fact, he showed himself ready to extend his travels to any future national campaign he might undertake.

The only difference was in his physical mobility, not in his endurance. They had to roll or lift him up to the podium, but from then on he stood up. Even though he wore leg braces and used a buckled strap across his back to steady him and free his hands, once he got into his speech you really couldn't tell that he was paralyzed at all.

His speeches were just as long as ever, and he spoke as many times a day as he had before. Had it been necessary, he could have campaigned daily, but he knew it was not. And he preferred to devote his weekdays to governing the state rather than campaigning.

As always, he proved a good judge of the voters' mood. With six candidates running against him, including ex-Governor Jim Folsom, to whom he was now related by marriage, he won 64 percent of the vote and didn't have to go into a runoff.

At that point the chairman of the Alabama Republican party indicated that he realized the futility of a Republican running against Dad in the fall. But Dad knew there was still a race to be run, and campaigned in the fall as energetically—and as successfully—as he had in the spring, to become the first Governor in Alabama history to win a second consecutive term under the state's 1968 succession law. On November 5, 1974, he won 476,724 votes to 83,502 cast for his Republican opponent, former State Sen. Elvin McCary, who had been repudiated by his own party leaders—a stunning five-to-one victory.

The night Dad won the spring primary by such an overwhelming margin, I was at his election headquarters, and I sensed something new in the air. I felt that the victory celebrants were projecting their thoughts toward something *beyond* the Gubernatorial race. They were thinking of the 1976 Presidential election.

For the 1974 elections seemed to be a mandate by the people. His condition had nothing to do with the way they voted. I think they voted for the man and what he has done—and what he is capable of doing.

I saw that all during his primary campaign. There was a fuel shortage at the time, and gas prices were high. So it was hard for people to get out. Yet the crowds were as big as ever. And as I shook hands with people, I could see they were emotional about the man in a more impressive way than ever before.

It's not that the people of Alabama are just *for* George Wallace. They *love* him. I know, because I had people come up to me constantly and say, "We just *love* your daddy!"

When you consider that he has been governing the state most of the time since 1963—though part of that time it was as Mother's adviser—his continued popularity is even more remarkable.

For in politics, in many cases no matter what kind of a job the man is doing, people tend to get tired of the same face. And they'll *certainly* let him know if he has done anything *wrong*. But Alabamians haven't tired or disapproved of George Wallace. His administrations have been honest and above board, and he has remained a true spokesman for the people. That's why the Wallace name on the ballot has been successful four times in a row—a truly exceptional record.

My own personal feeling about his future is that he *will* be involved in the 1976 Presidential campaign. As far as his remaining in the Democratic party, that remains to be seen. If they don't move back toward the center, I can see a third party emerging, led by my dad. But I don't really see how the Democrats can expect to win without him on the ticket—and without him on the ticket in the *first* spot, not the second spot.

Dad's supporters are already working in the Democratic party at the local level all around the country to build the kind of organization and support that will elect convention delegates for him in 1976. That's what the followers of Sen. George McGovern did in their successful campaign to win him the Democratic Presidential nomination in 1972, and we can all learn from their success. Ironically, we've been meeting with opposition from the same element that nominated Senator McGovern in 1972. But I hope the Democrats realize this time that you can't run roughshod over the people as the McGovernites did once they reached Miami in 1972. They had been great at organizing, but then they threw it all away. And if the Democrats fail to heed the voice of the people in 1976, then the people will reject them again, as they did in November of 1972, when the Democrats lost forty-nine states.

So we're trying to build our strength from the precincts up in 1976, which we didn't do in sufficient numbers in 1972, because we weren't as well organized as we are now. Whether the Democratic party responds and chooses George Wallace as its Presidential candidate remains to be seen. But I'm optimistic.

My own participation in Dad's campaigns has changed, however, in keeping with a change in my own life. I did not sing or play the guitar at his rallies in 1974. For one thing, I felt I could do more good by really mixing with the crowds, shaking hands and meeting the people.

And I didn't feel I could get up on stage and play the intimate, highly personal songs I've been writing lately and expect the audience to get *into* those tunes, because they weren't there for that. They were there for a political rally. And I'd be fooling myself and them, too, trying to play the songs I've written. Yet I did not want to go back to the lively, up-tempo country songs I used to play at Dad's rallies.

As a matter of fact, I'm not performing in public at all at present. I'm concentrating on writing and recording

my own songs. Here is one of the lyrics I've been working on.

> Let us stand hard here together.
> Let us reach for every dream.
> Let us find what has been written
> Behind their smoke-filled screens.
> May our courage never leave us.
> May we always stand for right
> And the truth shine down upon them
> To give the blind their sight.
> When you find your mind is playing
> Games with all the crowds,
> Then reach beyond their limits
> To seek what can be found.
> In our search for understanding
> We must first look to ourselves,
> For the knowledge has been written
> And awaits our souls to tell
> The message of the truth,
> The finding of our lives.

My college studies really don't permit me to take
the time to perform in any case. After I graduate we'll see
what happens.

And yet, although I've stopped performing for Dad's
campaigns, my music has recently been concerned with
my father—and with the memory of my mother. For in
1974 I recorded songs I'd written about them. The song
about Dad is called *Singer of His Song*. And the song
about Mother is called *She Walks In*. Both were issued on
the same record by MGM and were produced by Mike
Curb, the former president of the company, who has re-

mained very interested in my career, and by Harley Hatcher and Michael Lloyd.

These two songs were a complete musical expression of my feelings about my parents, and writing and performing them was deeply fulfilling to me.

Lately Dad and I spend a lot more time together sitting and talking, and that has made us much closer than we've ever been before.

Our discussions have been considerably deeper since my return to school. One day we talked about the new generation's feelings regarding technology—their belief that the individual has been forgotten in our technocratic society. It was something that had come up in my philosophy class, and Dad was very interested. He agreed that the individual in certain instances *has* been forgotten, and that we need to get back to a more personal relationship with people in their work.

And we've discussed our personal feelings about each other as they came up—the kind of feelings Dad has expressed in the introduction to this book, and which I have voiced in the book itself. This would not have been possible a few years ago. But now there's a real intimacy between us, and we're able to put it into words.

Dad realizes that I've grown up and learned a lot about life in general after having led a rather sheltered childhood and adolescence living in the Governor's Mansion. And he has found, as I have, that a strong bond grows between a father and a son when the son reaches maturity.

We usually talk in his bedroom or his therapy room, which is adjacent to it, when I come home from class. I have a morning class and an afternoon class, and I can see him while he's resting and during his therapy sessions.

When people talk to me about my father, perhaps the one subject that interests them most is the exact state of his health. "How does he feel?" they ask me.

I'm happy to say that his pain is 95 percent gone.

A major improvement in this area came about when he started receiving acupuncture treatments late in 1972 from a doctor from Taiwan. He took them for several months.

Until then he had suffered a great deal of abdominal pain, which not only caused him discomfort throughout the day but also interfered with his sleep. As soon as this pain was eased to a large degree through the acupuncture treatments, he not only felt better but the added hours of sleep improved his health.

His daily therapy at the Mansion includes walking on crutches with the aid of leg braces. Although in public he is generally in a wheelchair except when giving a speech, at home it's an increasingly common occurrence to have him walking on crutches through his therapy room, his bedroom and along the hallways of the upstairs living quarters. And of course weight lifting and walking along the parallel bars remain important parts of his therapy.

At one point it was thought he had some feeling in his lower legs, but that was just a reflex movement of his toes and was not voluntary. Although his spinal cord was not severed by the bullet that lodged in his spinal column, the tremendous trauma to the delicate nerves in the area that was caused by the bullet was responsible for the paralysis of the lower half of his body.

Although he believes it is possible that he *may* walk again, he has never said to me, "I think I'll walk again."

But you have to realize the way his mind works, and what he expects of himself. If you know my father, you just know that if it's possible in any way, he *will* walk some-day. And he doesn't have to say so. He just *feels* that.

With the great improvement in his physical condi-tion, his spirit is really up. Although he still has some slight pain ever so often, it's *very* slight. As a result, he spends more and more time outdoors as he becomes more active and energetic. They've just built a swimming pool in the back of the Mansion, and it's shaped like the state of Alabama. Dad will be spending a good deal of time in the pool, I'm sure, and this should help ease his remaining discomfort.

As I look back over my life as the son of two Gover-nors, I realize there was a time when being in this unique position really had me confused. But now it's like I've come out of the shadows into the light, and I can look back and see how so much that has happened to my family and me has been beneficial. Because there's really no way you can be involved and associated with *people* and not learn something. Lord knows, if we've been in-volved with *anything,* it's been people.

And people have been good to me and to our family. It's really quite an inspiration when people have the faith in your family that they've had in ours.

Looking back, my only deep regrets are my mother's death and my father's injury. Otherwise I can't see a thing I would really change.

I was reading the other day in Dad's room. I'd been playing tennis with my good friend, Ronnie Wise. And I asked Dad, "Why don't you come down and play tennis with us sometime? You hit it pretty good one day when you were out there playing, you know." He had played in his wheelchair, and a photo had appeared in a national magazine.

And he said, "Well, I might, Son, if I get a chance."

And I told him that I realized how busy he'd been when I was growing up, and how dedicated he'd been to what he was doing, and that he'd really never had a *lot* of time to spend with us. And I knew that he always regretted that he *didn't* have the time.

I also told him—the time was just right—I told him that I realized now what he was trying to do, and that I would have had it no other way. And he told me that he appreciated that.

When I think about my life, I'm really grateful. Because I had a beautiful mother and I have an outstanding father. And who could ask for more?

Index